THE
BUSINESS
OF LOVE

THE BUSINESS OF LOVE

9 Best Practices for Improving the Bottom Line of Your Relationship

Dr. John Curtis

IOD Press

For more information about this title, please contact:
IOD Press
1000 Winderley Place #147
Maitland, FL 32751-4171
(407) 265-6111
www.thebusinessoflove.org

Book design by Arbor Books
www.arborbooks.com

Printed in the United States

Library of Congress Control Number: 2005908638
ISBN: 0-9773444-0-1

Dedication

One of the most important lessons about relationships which I have learned over the years is that we are attracted to people who are similar to us in their level of intellect, emotional maturity and spiritual growth. With the supposed accuracy of hindsight, it is only natural to analyze those whom we have left behind in failed relationships as poor, troubled, and dysfunctional souls who did not deserve to be in a relationship with us.

The truth of the matter is that—more often than not—we were in these relationships because we were equally as troubled, but just couldn't see it. If you can accept this painful truth, you may also be able to break through to the realization this knowledge can reveal: the key to a happy, healthy intimate relationship is not to *find* the right person, but to *be* the right person.

After years of effort and a huge investment of time and money, I finally became the right person. And guess what? The most neurosis-free, kind, warm, loving, beautiful, and accepting woman I have ever known showed up in my life and agreed to marry me. I *found* the right person by focusing on *being* the right person.

I want to acknowledge my wife Charlotte for being there for me at the moment I was finally ready to be in the kind of relationship I had been pursuing for years with all the wrong women.

I dedicate this book to her, for proving to me that the struggle is worth it, because the reward is real!

Acknowledgements

I have so many people to thank for the role they have played in helping me write this book. In most cases, they do not know it and probably never will. From childhood until now, I have been shaped and molded by forces and factors that I could never have predicted (and certainly cannot take credit for). While it is often easy to look back at life and wish that certain things had never happened, I can honestly say that I like who I am today. If anything in my history were changed, the outcome would also change. So let's not try to tinker with the past (as if we could) but simply accept it.

More specifically, after moving into adulthood and true self-sufficiency, I am now doing something very different than what I started out doing. I began my career as a marriage and family counselor. Then, after many years, I transitioned into my current career as an organizational development consultant. This book has helped me to bridge those two worlds and to see the direct connection between marital satisfaction and sound business principles.

So, without trying to list everyone who has ever had an impact on me and my thinking throughout this transition, I do want to acknowledge and thank my professors, mentors, and colleagues. I also, especially, want to thank my parents and sisters who are a vital part of those forces and factors that made me who I am today. I want to thank Charlene for helping me in the earliest stages of developing the proposal for this book and Becky, Claire, Jordan, Judy, Kathleen and Paul for helping me with the final stages. Most important, I want to thank Nicole Westmoreland for her insights, energy, and enthusiasm for this book as well as the invaluable contributions she made in helping write *The Business of Love*. Finally, I want to thank Arbor Books for the support, advice and guidance that made it possible to bring this book into being.

Table of Contents

THE
BUSINESS
OF LOVE

Chapter 1—Introduction

*"A friendship founded on business is better than
a business founded on friendship."*
—John D. Rockefeller—great American industrialist

What made you pick up this book? Did the words "business" and "love" together strike you as contradictory? Was it so unexpected that you had to see what was inside, or did the title strike you as an ingenious approach to relationships? Regardless, you might be looking for a radically different approach to your relationship, or perhaps you just need a new twist on an old theme. If you are like most people, I bet you've had your share of good and bad relationships. You are most likely in one or the other right now, and you may be full of questions about what to do to either sustain or change it. Well, you've come to the right place.

Depending upon where you live, your age, and other demographic variables, the odds that your current or future relationships will be successful are only average at best, as shown in the table of divorce statistics below:

- State with the lowest divorce rate: Massachusetts. Rate per 1,000 population: 2.4
- State with the highest divorce rate: Nevada. Rate per 1,000 population: 6.8
- Percentage of population that is married: 53.8% (down from 62% in 1990, 72% in 1970)
- Percentage of population that has never married: 28%
- Percentage of population that is divorced: 9.7% (up from 8% in 1990, 6% in 1980)
- Median age at first marriage: Males: 26.9 Females: 25.3
- Median age at first divorce: Males: 30.5 Females: 29
- Median age at second marriage: Males: 34 Females: 32
- Median age at second divorce: Males: 39.3 Females: 37
- Median duration of first marriages that end in divorce: Males: 7.8 years Females: 7.9 years
- Median duration of second marriages that end in divorce: Males: 7.3 years Females: 6.8 years
- Median number of years people wait to remarry after their first divorce: Males: 3.3 years Females: 3.1 years

INTRODUCTION

- Percentage of married people who reach their 5th, 10th, and 15th anniversaries: 5th: 82% 10th: 65% 15th: 52%

- Percentage of married people who reach their 25th, 35th, and 50th anniversaries: 25th: 33% 35th: 20% 50th: 5%

- Percentage of people who have ever been married by the age of 25: Males: 32% Females: 50%

- Percentage of people who have ever been married by the age of 35: Males: 77% Females: 84%

- Percentage of people who have ever been married by the age of 45: Males: 87% Females: 90%

- Percentage of people who have ever been married by the age of 55: Both males and females: 95%

Adapted from Kreider, Rose M., 2005. Number, Timing, and Duration of Marriages and Divorces: 2001. Current Population Reports, P70-97. U.S. Census Bureau, Washington, DC. *Parts from* Divorce Magazine, viewed 7/26/05 at http://www.divorcemag.com/statistics/statsUS.shtml

Perhaps you are thinking that you are better than average and can defy those odds. Or maybe you've come from a family of divorced people and know firsthand the potential pitfalls of marriage. The main point is that, no matter what brought you to this place, you may be interested in a totally new approach that will enable you to avoid common problems associated with both building and enhancing *any* long-term, committed relationship.

If history teaches us anything, it is that none of the existing ways of building relationships fully addresses the realities of love and marriage in the 21st century. There's got to be a better way, and that better way is what this book is about.

The approach I am proposing is focused on applying proven business strategies to the ongoing development of your long-term, committed and intimate relationship. While the idea of using business strategies in your intimate relationship may seem cold and impersonal, or even offensive, this book is all about intimacy. Nothing destroys a loving relationship faster than power struggles, unresolved conflict, feelings of inequity and the realization that you both have a very different vision for the future of your relationship. This book says some very unconventional things, and says them in a brand new way that you've likely never considered before. Think this book's central idea is bizarre or crazy? Well, the alternative is to play the odds and take your chances by basing the most important relationship in your life on one of the following historic models of marriage.

Marriage Models

The earliest model for marriage was one of *Means*. Men and women joined together because it made economic or political sense, and the decision was often based on a family's or tribe's need to survive. Love, romance and personal affection had little to do with this bond. The families decided the most important issues, such as matters of land, goats, inheritance, children, religion and dowries. They arranged marriages based on how the pairing would affect the means or resources of the family, village or kingdom. Little thought or concern was shown for what the couple might have desired.

Unbelievably, marriages of Means still happen today in America. My wife's hairdresser, Alessandra, is a 36-year-old woman from Italy. Based on family tradition, while she was living in the U.S., the fathers arranged for her to marry Nick, an Italian tile layer from her village. Their fathers determined that this would be the best way to ensure that the couple would have the means to earn a good living in the U.S., so they could support both families by sending supplements back home to Italy.

The first time she met her husband-to-be, she thought, "He's awfully short." She said that it was ten years into the marriage before she actually fell in love with her "pre-selected" spouse, and only after returning to visit his family in Italy, where she saw how poorly the other men treated their wives. She counts herself lucky. This is a rare success.

Next is the *Fantasy* model, where a marriage is based on romantic love alone. This model is not driven by means or economic necessity. In fact, it's often quite the opposite, and parents are frequently opposed to such unions. Its foundation is much less practical, and is defined by the illusion that "all you need is love!" This model of marriage is very much alive today, and was likely the basis for your first "serious" relationship. Movies and television continue to portray simplistic, one-dimensional, and often completely unrealistic images of what our relationships are supposed to look like. In addition, Hollywood continues to provide us with almost laughable tabloid relationships that seemingly form and dissolve overnight. Celebrities living in a self-centered, overindulgent fantasy world are probably not good role models on which to base your marriage.

In addition, fantasy marriages are often a form of escape. Many women and men see marriage as a way out of a troubled home, the fear of being alone, financial pressure, or even another marriage. All too often, fantasy marriages begin with the end in mind... the end to all the problems a person had before getting married. The obvious pitfall is that, once you have made your escape, the purpose of the marriage is over. Basing a marriage on avoiding something unpleasant is a prerequisite for divorce. It is like avoiding pressure at work by drinking heavily, or ignoring financial problems by going shopping. This approach to marriage is not sustainable.

The third or *Traditional* model is what you likely grew up with and is something of a combination of a marriage of means disguised with fantasy-style love and, perhaps, a dose of religion. Our parents fell in love, got married, and then set about building a relationship based on economic need, religious beliefs and some pretty traditional attitudes about what women and men were supposed to do in the marriage. If you are a member of the Senior Generation, or even in the early part of the Baby Boom Generation there were a lot of conventional assumptions such as:

- Men worked outside the home for the same company until retirement.
- Women stayed at home and raised 3.2 children until the last one left home, and then continued in their parental roles as grandmothers.

- The husband knew best and therefore managed the money.
- The wife was in charge of the family's social life.
- Sex was in the male-superior position.
- They all were supposed to live happily ever after.

Then, beginning in the late 1960s, America experienced tremendous social upheavals. The women's movement exploded, and male earning power eroded, transforming their roles forever. However, if you are a member of the X or Y Generations, the marriage model is still typically traditional, but the assumptions have changed significantly, such as:

- Both parents work for multiple employers over their employment history.
- Families are having fewer children and childless marriages are more common.
- Children are in day care or are latchkey kids.
- Divorce is commonplace and acceptable.
- Extended families have been eroded by our mobile society.
- Technology has transformed our lives and accelerated our pace.
- Blended families of yours, mine and ours have become typical.

In a single generation, dual-income marriages have gone from being rare to being the norm. Currently, dual-income couples—with both the husband and wife working outside the home—make up over 60% of all households in America.

Stay-at-home moms in single-income families are now the exception. These dual-income couples are faced with the typical pressures that can affect any marriage in our modern society, along with a unique set of challenges that neither our parents nor any other generation in U.S. history have ever had to face.

As a result—and quite understandably—fewer people are getting married now than at any time in our nation's history. The national marriage rate has dropped over 40% in the past four decades, and, on average, nearly half of those who do get married will eventually split up. In addition, young adults are delaying marriage until later than ever, with the average age of marriage for men rising to over 27, and for women to over 25. Worse still, only 30% of females and 40% of males believe that married couples are happier than those who stay single. The trend away from marriage is clear and quite unsettling.

"It is not the strongest of the species that survive, nor the most intelligent, but the one most responsive to change."—Charles Darwin

None of these earlier relationship models—Means, Fantasy, or Traditional—is inherently good or bad, and each has some merit. It is just that none of them is responsive to changing conditions and, as a result, each has become outmoded, irrelevant and often simply don't work. Consider that, in the general population, you have roughly a 50%

chance of having a successful marriage. Who would want to start a new venture faced with such poor odds? These models are in danger of extinction and simply are not in tune with life in 21st century America, with our global economy, unparalleled advances in technology, post-9/11 and hurricane anxieties, middle-income stagnation, and unprecedented demands on marriage and child rearing. If there were ever a time for a new model for relationships, it is now.

THE BUSINESS OF LOVE MODEL

"Success comes from good judgment; good judgment comes from experience; experience comes from bad judgment!"
—Rita Mae Brown—author

Building a relationship that actually works in today's world means learning from the history of bad judgment in marriage… your own or others. The institution of marriage has changed more in the past few decades than it has in thousands of years. If you want to build a relationship of the future in the middle of this transformation, you will have to be a historian and a pioneer. You must learn from the past and you must courageously go where no one has gone before, using a radically different approach.

This radical new approach for building relationships is the *Business* model that is illustrated at the end of this chapter. Just as successful organizations are grounded in established principles and sound practices, so too can a satisfying relationship reap emotional profits using the same proven business approach. For example, one common business practice has to do with the importance of having clear expectations about what is anticipated of us on the job. Most employees expect job descriptions that provide clarity, focus, direction and the specifics of the job, along with some form of documentation that spells out what they will be paid and how they will be evaluated in the future. It would be very frustrating—if not impossible—for the average person to perform his or her job without knowing what was expected and how they would be evaluated. Yet love-struck couples, living in a fantasy world, hope their relationships will fall into place and last forever. They do so without the benefit of clear expectations, because they lack a job description. Most work/life balance studies show that conflicts about money, children and household chores are the top sources of marital conflict. Worse still, without any agreement as to task requirements or performance expectations, each partner often gives the other daily criticism that only makes matters worse, such as: "I can't believe you spent money on that! Do you think money grows on trees?" or "You're no better a parent than your father was!" or "Why is the house such a mess?"

This book is about using good judgment based on experience to avoid these mistakes inherent in the failing relationship models of the past. More importantly, it is about what you *can* do to be successful and prosper in your relationship by using a totally new model for building a relationship. This book does not delve into your past, analyze your parents, or explore all your neuroses—it does not provide psychotherapy. It is one of those rare books for normal people like you and me.

Is This Book Right For You?

Anybody can use this new *Business* relationship model, even if you have little or no experience actually working in the business world. In addition, concepts and activities in this book can be successfully applied to a budding romance or a new marriage or to validate and strengthen a relationship that has lasted decades. This book can even provide answers about why previous relationships failed and how your experience of those setbacks can actually improve your judgment in making better relationship choices now. The business model is simple and straightforward, but I want to caution you—applying it to your relationship may not be easy and may even be unsettling at times. But the activities in this book can also be fun and energizing, as you and your partner embark on this process of self-discovery and explore various aspects of your relationship. Enjoy the journey!

This book builds on successful concepts used every day in business that (believe it or not) translate directly to your relationship to increase the honesty, deepen the commitment and protect the romance. You can improve the bottom line of your relationship if you approach it as a business. To help bring these business strategies to life in personal relationships, each chapter begins with a letter describing an actual relationship challenge that the chapter will address. I believe this question-and-answer format provides a real-world understanding of how business strategies can be successfully applied to a wide range of relationship issues. There is much to profit from when you build a world-class relationship based on sound best practices!

After reading this book, you will gain a whole new perspective on how to think about a relationship and its basis, through activities such as discussing the long-term vision of your relationship. With this philosophical framework in mind, you will then get a chance to learn about and work through concrete issues such as setting measurable objectives, funding and branding the relationship, developing job descriptions, giving productive relationship feedback, establishing your benefits and compensation (yes, even in an intimate relationship, you deserve an "emotional paycheck"), and conducting relationship meetings and retreats. (In fact, if you want to jump to Chapter 7 on job descriptions and get right into the concrete issues, go ahead. You won't be lost if you are the kind of person who likes to work through practical issues first.) This book will help couples:

- Find a clear and common vision of an ideal future state for the relationship

- Develop a comprehensive set of measurable objectives that define why the relationship exists, where it is headed and how you will measure success

- Determine attitudes about money and their role in successfully funding the marital enterprise

- Develop a relationship logo and market a unified relationship brand

- Learn how to deal with the consequences of mergers and acquisitions in the context of couples and families

- Create clear job descriptions that pinpoint each partner's roles and responsibilities

- Design a relationship feedback process complete with tips on regular appraisal sessions

- Establish a compensation and benefits "package" that tangibly supports and reinforces your relationship job description and underscores each partner's contributions toward achieving the vision and objectives of the relationship

- Learn how to hold regular relationship meetings and retreats where the partners can step back from the relationship and objectively review their progress toward their vision, and then develop new strategies to support their objectives

Maybe you are not business-minded—or perhaps you think that these business-based strategies seem a bit too "cut-and-dry." I assure you that the relationship activities and exercises set out in this book and the separate Workbook are presented in a fun and energizing format. Couples at any stage in their relationship can learn how to create a foundation and structure where romance, authenticity, intimacy and a sense of true friendship can flourish. This can be accomplished without the problems that typically undermine relationships founded on the failed models of the past. If you are still not convinced and do not see the connection between business and intimate relationships, I would like to offer the following for your serious consideration. Most of us would be hard-pressed to describe the specific strategies we use daily or the number of hours spent weekly to maintain and improve our most important intimate relationship. However, on the other hand, if you are a full-time employee, you spend at least 2,080 hours a year performing tasks to help your employer maintain and improve his or her bottom line. You are likely performing those tasks for an organization that has some type of business plan that includes a vision and measurable objectives. In addition, you probably have a job description, receive some form of performance feedback, and know something about how the business does salary planning—and this is all for an employer that you are likely to leave in just a few years.

Given that most of us enter marriage with the assumption of permanence, and coupling this with our ever-increasing life expectancies, it is likely you could spend ten, twenty, thirty years or more with the same person. Don't you think that a relationship that could last that long deserves the same time, energy and commitment that you give to your employer? This is what the book is about: applying proven best practices from business to achieve a world-class relationship. I assure you that the return on your investment will be well worth the effort.

The Business of Love Relationship Model

As the following model shows, building a relationship based on a business model involves two separate but linked components:

STRATEGIC: *Relating to the identification of long-term aims and interests, and the means of achieving them.* Chapters 2 through 6 focus on the Strategic best practices for building a successful relationship.

TACTICAL: *Relating to or involving actions carefully planned and executed to achieve a specific result.* Chapters 7 through 10 focus on the Tactical best practices for sustaining a successful relationship.

The Business of Love Model

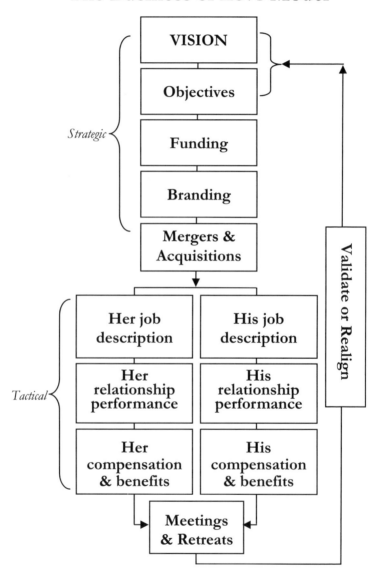

STRATEGIC: *Relating to the identification of long-term aims and interests, and the means of achieving them!*

Chapter 2—Creating the Vision of Your Relationship— Best Practice #1

"The best way to plan for the future is to create it."
—Peter Drucker—writer, economist, management consultant and university professor

Chapter Objectives:

1. Understand the role of a vision statement and its importance in relationship development.
2. Learn how to write a relationship vision statement.
3. Resolve differences in relationship vision statements.
4. Build a unified vision statement for your relationship.

Dear John,

I've been married for three years to a wonderful woman I've known for just over ten years. While I love her very much, I have recently discovered some differences between us that I can see turning into a mushroom cloud in the future. I am what you'd call a "dreamer" and a "planner." I have all of these long-range ideas for how I see my life and my wife's life. For example, I want to save money for a boat that we would sail together for some extended cruises.

Unfortunately, my wife doesn't look at the future—our future—in the same way. She's a day-to-day kind of person, who likes things just the way they are. She has always looked at my plans as a nice dream, but when it comes to realistically planning it out, she loses interest.

What can I do to align our plans for the future, and get her interested in shared dreams?

Signed,
A Hopeful Sailor
Marathon, FL

The ideal state of your relationship

Historically, marriages based on means, fantasy, or tradition did not include any long-range planning on how to achieve the ideal relationship. It is quite amazing how many smart people just assume that somehow the marriage will magically work out. As it has been said,

"Love is blind, and marriage is an institution for the blind."
—James Graham—author

In most cases, couples simply and blindly "wing it" as they move though the predictable phases of any long-term, intimate relationship, starting with romance, then followed by commitment which is a prelude for the predictable conflict phase. Then, if they are fortunate enough to successfully make it through the turmoil of the conflict phase, they may achieve true intimacy... where they know everything about their partner but still love them anyway and where they share the same vision for the relationship!

This is the issue with our Hopeful Sailor. Though the couple has known each other for ten years, they have not created a shared, long-term vision for their future *together*. Regardless of what stage your relationship may be in now, it can still greatly benefit from applying the solid business principle and best practice of sound, long-range vision planning.

Just like enlightened executives and entrepreneurs who create and continually refine a long-range strategic plan for their business, you and your partner can develop and continually update your own plan for how your relationship will develop and sustain its "profitability." Your vision should have a long time "horizon" and might not change over a period of decades. I often consult with businesses to help them develop a vision to focus and define where their business is headed. Developing this shared vision for your relationship will make it much easier to focus on the more tactical, concrete elements of relationships that will be covered in later chapters.

The work of this chapter will begin with writing the

vision statement for your relationship: a few words that define your future ideal state of your relationship. But first, let's look at some examples of vision statements that are not about intimate relationships but are simple and easy to grasp, like "a world without hunger, or war or disease!" Another example is our own Pledge of Allegiance to the Flag…"One nation, under God, indivisible, with liberty and justice for all." As you can see, a vision statement can be basic or bold, idealistic, grand, easy to understand, and sometimes poetic. It should motivate, inspire, and stimulate.

Now, to become a bit more focused, the following demonstrate how some familiar organizations describe their vision.

At Microsoft, we work to help people and businesses throughout the world realize their full potential. As a company, and as individuals, we value:

- Integrity and honesty.
- Passion for customers, for our partners, and for technology.
- Openness and respectfulness.
- Taking on big challenges and seeing them through.
- Constructive self-criticism, self-improvement, and personal excellence.
- Accountability to customers, shareholders, partners, and employees for commitments, results, and quality.

Special Olympics: is an unprecedented global movement which, through quality sports training and competition, improves the lives of people with intellectual disabilities and, in turn, the lives of everyone they touch.

Pfizer: "We dedicate ourselves to humanity's quest for longer, happier lives through innovation in pharmaceutical, consumer and animal health products."

Writing your vision statement

Now, after seeing some examples, you can better understand vision statements and how to write your own—so let's get to work. Your vision statement describes a future ideal state of your relationship. It is often stated in expressive, bold and poetic terms—a combination of values, ideals, goals, expectations, beliefs, possibilities, and the unique contributions each of you will bring to the relationship throughout your lives.

First, I recommend that you and your partner work on the first draft of your vision statements individually. Begin by writing a version or two that describe, in a few words, *your* vision for the relationship, before being influenced or biased by what your partner might write. This approach also helps to ensure that one partner does not avoid this challenging task or give in to the other partner's vision in order to "keep the peace."

Remember, this is your life, too! The success of your relationship is due, in part, to what you add to the relationship, not what you give up to be in it!

Next, decide on a time and place to discuss your vision statement with your partner. If your partner is not reading this book then, at a minimum, ask them to think about it and be prepared to discuss it. Tell your partner how important it is to you to jointly develop a shared vision to help plan for and ensure a long-term, successful relationship. As is often said in business, "Those who fail to plan,

plan to fail," so don't let this be the case with your intimate relationship.

Once you both have made the commitment to this task, block out some time to work on this activity and set a deadline when you will share vision statements in preparation for combining them into a unified vision for the relationship. You'll need time to truly think about your vision of the future. The mental process of creating the vision statement forces you and your partner to stop and wonder, "What *is* my long-term view of our relationship? I never thought about that before. I'm simply in love and want to spend the rest of my life with this person." Well, okay, that's all fine and good, but is it enough to make a relationship last? In case you missed it, go back and read the first chapter of this book to remind yourself why "simply being in love" is rarely enough anymore to make the relationship last.

This is where the hard work comes in. Tread slowly and carefully, because this is the first of several activities throughout this book that may be difficult, sometimes unsettling and yet deeply rewarding. Working to develop a common vision that you and your partner fully support is the first and usually the most difficult hurdle. Early in the process of developing a vision statement, it is likely that you'll think of a vision for you "yourself" rather than for you and your partner. Or you may find out that your vision statement appears to be quite different than your partner's vision for the relationship. You may have some major issues to discuss!

That's okay. It is simply part of the process of moving from a single view of the future to one of a couple working in a unified partnership.

Imagine your ideal relationship ten, twenty, thirty or more years into the future, and envision where you would like your relationship to be, what you and your partner will be doing, what achievements you will have made, what your sense of purpose will be, and so forth. Based on this mental image, begin to write a first draft of a vision statement for your relationship. Keep in mind that it is very unlikely that you will write the ideal statement at first. It is okay to use phases, change the wording, and do lots of editing… just get started, but be sure to use a pencil with a good eraser or be prepared to make many changes in the statement on your computer. *Vision statement worksheets and guidelines are available in the Workbook that accompanies this book that can be found at www.thebusinessoflove.org*

Getting started—"warm-up" exercises

Exercise # 1—Before you begin writing a vision statement, you might want to do a little pre-work to help you with this task in case nothing immediately comes to mind. You may want to identify some of your core values to incorporate into your vision statement. One way to spot these is to look for tangible items in your life that represent the things you value most. It may be a piece of jewelry you're wearing, an emblem on your key chain, a picture on your computer desktop, or a cherished symbol on the wall.

Typically, these items represent or remind you of something of great value to you… a religious icon, a beloved grandparent, a significant life accomplishment and so on. A vision statement for your relationship might incorporate these core values, and you may find it easier to begin writing your vision once you have pinpointed tangible items that you treasure.

Exercise # 2—Consider doing a search on the Internet for other examples of vision statements. Go to websites of organizations that you know and trust… consider the website of your employer (if one exists), or your place of worship, a community hospital, your favorite electronics brand, your alma mater or even a branch of local or state government. Many examples are readily available, and viewing how others have written vision statements may help you develop a better vision statement for your relationship.

Writing your vision statements

Look at the following examples of two seemingly different vision statements from the same couple. Each partner created her or his statement separately.

Hers:

In our ideal life, we will express our individuality through our intelligence and creativity. We are equal partners in our relationship, but value each other's different approach to life. We are close to God and active in our Church. We do all this with the intention of being truthful with ourselves and each other and by enriching our lives and leaving the world a better place. We will travel, expand our horizons, deepen family relationships and live life to the fullest, free of materialistic burdens.

His:

My vision for the future ideal state of our relationship is one based on integrity and full of rich and deep meaning that comes from ever increasing exploration of who we are and how we show our love. We each will be devoted to helping the other reach their full potential. We will give our children roots and wings, and always laugh and learn with them. We will achieve financial serenity and maintain balance in all areas of life together.

You can see that the couple has different perspectives, but once the visions are shared and integrated, they may be closer in meaning than they seem. Look for the commonalities in concepts and values, regardless of the words. Are you using synonymous terms that sound different on the surface but are really saying the same basic thing? You may be talking about the value of "integrity" while your partner emphasizes "truth." Can you see how they are similar and resolvable when examined side by side? When you identify core concepts and values within each vision statement, you might find that you are closer to each other than you thought.

Also, don't be concerned if your vision statements sound *completely* different than these examples. There is no right way to do this, and no pre-determined outcome. The key is to be bold, honest, creative and future-focused with an emphasis on the *ideal* state you desire for your relationship.

Combining your vision statements

What you are looking for in this part of the activity can be compared to the lighting of a unity candle at a wedding ceremony. Have you ever seen this ritual at a wedding or did you use it at your own? As you may know, it begins with each partner lighting an individual candle. Together, the couple then lights the single unity candle with their individual candles and then extinguishes their separate candles, thus taking two separate flames and making them one. This is a symbol of joining your individual visions into one common vision for the relationship.

Here is an example of combining the separate vision statements from above!

Our vision for our relationship is one where we will have complete trust and honesty, free of fears or anxieties and full of acceptance and support. We each will be devoted to helping one another reach our full potential through the ever-increasing exploration of who we are as partners and parents, and by expressing our individuality. We will be close to God, who will bless us with lives full of deep meaning. We will continue to explore our world and include our family whenever possible. We will be free of material burdens while living a rich and full life.

A word on compromise and negotiation!

Throughout this book, two types of core personal issues that can lead to potential conflicts in any relationship will be discussed: *needs and values*. Needs are often common desires or wishes that change over time and tend to be situational, like how you spend your free time, the type of clothes you wear, or how tidy you keep your bathroom. Values, on the other hand, are about those long established and difficult to change beliefs and ideals like our deeply held views of religion, money and politics.

Need conflicts can often be resolved through compromise… you can alternate who cleans the bathroom, or flip a coin to see whose turn it is to clean it, or buy a house with two bathrooms or hire a housekeeper.

However, when trying to combine your visions for the future of your relationship into a shared vision, you may run into values conflicts. It is often at this point, when you start to dig deeper into who you are and what you value in the relationship, that you discover new dimensions of your personality and that of your partner. This process of discovery can help you reach new levels of openness and intimacy that you never imagined possible. At the same time, you may find that you and your partner appear to be far apart on the values that each of you has for the vision of the relationship, and this is where the hard work of negotiating begins.

This process of negotiation is at the heart of *The Business of Love*. No matter how long it takes, I urge you to keep talking, discovering and working toward a common vision for the relationship despite what may at first seem like irreconcilable differences. These discussions may evoke strong emotions and require a concerted effort to stay open and accepting of each other.

Early in our marriage, when Charlotte and I would have what appeared to be a values conflict, I would get very passionate, which is typical of my negotiating style. I would sound very strong and forceful, but I later found out that Charlotte got scared and reacted by shutting down. Her style was to compromise to achieve peace at any price, so she did not "push back" or "stand her ground," which only frustrated me more because I wanted to negotiate to resolve the issue, not avoid it. Now, as she jokingly states when I get into my passionate mode, "oh that's just John!" She is not discounting me, but instead, she has learned that is my style and, with a little time, patience and understanding, we always work it through.

In addition, because of working on a vision for your relationship, your worst fear may seem to come true… you and your partner do not appear to be compatible. Certainly, not every relationship is meant to last. Because of poor judgment, you may have entered into a relationship that was doomed from the start. However, I urge you not to jump to conclusions now. Instead, keep exploring by reading about the other best practices described in this book until you make it all the way through. The doubt you might be feeling now may simply be the result of entering a new level of honesty with yourself and intimacy with your partner, so it is only natural to feel anxious and afraid.

Just remember not to "throw in the towel" to avoid anxiety or fear by compromising your values. Doing so may likely mean that you will grow increasingly angry with yourself and your partner as you give up more and more of who you are and what you believe in order to keep the peace... the result of negotiation in *The Business of Love* must be a win-win outcome.

If it seems too difficult a task to merge your separate visions, set them aside for now and move forward to a chapter on tactical strategies that may be more concrete and straightforward for you than this one. A good example of this is Chapter 7, which deals with "Job Descriptions." In that chapter, you will write job descriptions for yourself and your partner. You will likely find it easier to talk about more concrete issues such as who does the laundry, who does yard work, who manages finances, and who takes care of children. Don't panic! You can always come back to the vision statement and refine it once you have a better understanding of the more tangible aspects of your life together, or you can move on to Chapter 3 on writing objectives.

Chapter Highlights:

- *Translating the benefits of vision statements for organizations directly into improving a new or existing intimate relationship*

- *Aligning long-range values and expectations through a vision statement for the relationship*

- *Employing a vision statement as the standard by which all else in the relationship is measured*

STRATEGIC: *Relating to the identification of long-term aims and interests, and the means of achieving them!*

Chapter 3—Developing Your Relationship's Objectives— Best Practice #2

"The vision must be followed by the venture. It is not enough to stare up the steps—we must step up the stairs."
—Vance Havne

/bjectives:

ıderstand how to jointly develop relationıip objectives.

2. Identify and define the core dimensions of your relationship.

3. Set up measurable objectives for all dimensions of your relationship.

Dear John,

I am in a quandary with my fiancé. He has been a student of one subject or another for the four years I've known him, and he still doesn't know what he wants to do with his life. I have a lot of respect for his intelligence but I feel it's time he should get off the fence. He does not seem to have any definite ideas for his career, or where we might live, or our future together.

We are in our early thirties and I am ready to have kids, but I don't feel like I can bring children into the world when my husband has no job or aspiration toward employment. In fact, I'd eventually like to cut back my job to part-time so I can be around more for our children. Help!

Signed,
Future Wife of a Professional Student
Little Rock, Arkansas

First the what, now the how

By now, you may have a shared vision of what you and your partner would like your relationship to be in the future or have decided to develop one after reading more of this book. Next, it is time to create a series of measurable objectives that define the specific dimensions of your relationship. Just as many organizations write measurable objectives of what they want to achieve in the area of sales, profit, market share, customer or employee satisfaction and a wide variety of other outcomes, couples can also work collectively to write objectives that define their relationship outcomes.

Typically, objectives can help answer such questions as:

- What are we trying to achieve?

- What are our priorities?

- How do we want to use our resources?

- What measures will we use to determine success?

Unlike the vision statement, relationship objectives are narrow and specific and typically can be grouped into various dimensions that are a part of any relationship. Each dimension helps describe specific areas of activity within your relationship to identify what you both want to achieve in concrete and measurable terms.

Examples of Relationship Dimensions:

1) Family, 2) Fiscal, 3) Health & Wellness, 4) Intimacy, 5) Spirituality, 6) Leisure, 7) Career, 8) Life-Long Learning

The Future Wife of a Professional Student wants to know what their life is going to be like in Little Rock, or wherever they may live. She may feel that her fiancé has not decided, "what he wants to be when he grows up," nor does he seem to have a plan to answer that question anytime soon. If they would start on developing a set of objectives and categorize them in the relationship dimensions described in this chapter, their relationship might begin to have more focus and gain momentum.

Writing relationship objectives

While writing your vision statement was a solitary effort that you then shared and combined as a couple, objectives are best written together from the outset. You and your partner should agree on which dimensions described in this chapter such as family, fiscal or career fit your circumstances and are the most important to making your collective vision come true. This exercise will require a good deal of self-awareness, some negotiation and perhaps a bit of compromise.

After all, if you have an objective to buy a motorcycle and tour the country by the time you turn 40, and your husband is deathly afraid of motorcycles, you might have to settle for touring parts of the country by other means. But the objective is to tour the country, and perhaps you will do some of it in a camper, on a train or by car, or you may do some of it alone, on your motorcycle. It's okay to have solitary objectives intermingled with ones you both want to achieve. Single and joint objectives will be discussed in more depth later in this chapter.

Don't worry if some of the dimensions don't apply to you, or if you have trouble deciding what you want in any given dimension, or if you want to add some to the list. Life is fluid and dynamic; aspects of your objectives will be too. Unlike your vision statement, which has a time "horizon" that might not change over a period of decades, objectives may be shorter-term and might shift significantly once you achieve certain milestone objectives—such as getting married, having your first child, completing college, or building your first home—and move on to another stage in your lives.

This exercise is likely to be challenging and time-consuming, yet it is not to be hurried. Feel free to break the effort up into multiple meetings or sessions. Start with simply agreeing on the most important dimensions. In subsequent meetings, you can discuss the specific objectives and construct the details.

It is important to note that many of these dimensions are interconnected. For example, if your objective is to travel the country (Leisure), this objective will have economic implications (Fiscal). If your objective is to make company Vice President (Career), for which you need an MBA, this will affect both your continuing education (Life-Long Learning) and investment aspirations (Fiscal). You may find yourself moving from one dimension to another and back again. That's okay. It is more important to make sure each objective is as measurable, concrete and specific as you can make it.

The following **S.M.A.R.T.** guidelines, commonly used in business, might help you in writing objectives in each dimension. It is important that your objectives be:

- **S**pecific—Objectives are concrete and something you can actually plan for and work toward in a realistic manner.

- **M**easurable—You need to be able to note progress and determine whether you are getting closer to achieving your objective.

- **A**chievable—Objectives you develop for each dimension of the relationship are things that can actually be accomplished.

- **R**elevant—Be sure not to lose touch with reality. Ensure that the objective is tied to the dimension of your relationship which helps to define the reason the relationship exists.

- **T**ime-bound—Objectives have a specific and reasonable date by which you plan on accomplishing what you have committed to do, whether it is six months or six years into the future.

Dimensions of a relationship

So, let's begin looking at these different relationship dimensions. Start by asking yourselves, "What would you like to achieve for yourself and your relationship in any or all of the following dimensions?"

1) Family—If you're newly married and have no children, deciding on the number of children you want to have (if any) will be important. Some couples may bring children into a new marriage from a previous relationship, or they may choose to be adoptive or foster parents. For others, taking care of aging parents and raising children at the same time will be a major family issue. In the 21st century, the definition of "family" has changed dramatically. Co-habitation, same-sex marriage, foster children, bi-racial families, international adoption, elder care, and step-parents are just a few of the unique facets of what it means to be a contemporary family. Be sure to discuss specific objectives that you each have for the family dimension of your relationship.

While much may be beyond your control (like an aging but healthy parent who suddenly suffers a stroke and requires 24-hour attention and care), talking about what you and your partner would likely do if this situation were to arise can go a long way toward preventing a relationship crisis before it ever happens. In addition, discussing these types of issues helps you to learn more about your partner's values and priorities. For example, consider some of the following questions in just a few important areas of this dimension as a way to learn more about each other while developing greater intimacy with your partner:

1. Do you want children? How many? Would you adopt? Should they attend public, private or religious school, or be home-schooled? Who is to do the nurturing and the disciplining?

2. How will you spend the holidays? How do you feel about relatives visiting? How would you deal with a "problematic" sibling? Do you expect to visit family on vacations?

3. How would you deal with an aging parent? Would you consider having a senile parent move in? How much financial support would you provide a sick or troubled family member?

While there are many more issues that can arise in this dimension, don't overlook its importance because it is one area of a committed, intimate relationship that may require skillful negotiations, compromise or even sacrifice.

2) Fiscal—Have you dreamed of retiring at 50? Do you want to play the odds by investing in aggressive technology stocks or play it safe by investing in conservative bond funds? What kind of lifestyle do you hope to achieve in terms of the cars you drive, the home you live in, the clothes you wear, and the material items that you want to own. Maybe you want to take a trip around the world on a shoe-string budget or on an elegant and expensive cruise ship. Be sure to discuss financial objectives with your partner and how you see achieving those objectives. In addition, this area might include how you will finance objectives that have been identified in other dimensions, such as the cost of any further education, international travel, your children's college expenses and estate planning. At a minimum, this dimension might include an objective about when and how you will develop a detailed financial plan. Money is often, needlessly, a source of tension in an intimate relationship. However, in *The Business of Love*, advanced financial planning can be one of the most powerfully positive aspects of your intimate relationship. This dimension, too, may easily help you both match competencies and motivation with regard to financial planning that will be discussed later in the chapter on job descriptions

3) Health and Wellness—Do you want to be a tri-athlete, avoid an early heart attack, stop smoking, lose weight, or have liposuction? All of these involve developing specific objectives for the physical aspects of your relationship. Studies verify that healthier couples have happier relationships, and, conversely, that happily married couples live longer—especially men! Be sure to consider mental health as an area where you may want to set some specific objectives. As was stated in the introduction, this book is not meant to provide psychotherapy. It is written for normal people with typical relationship challenges. However, just as with learning to overcome poor health habits, you might need to set an objective in this dimension to address all the phobias or compulsions that you have developed. Unfortunately, some people have suffered trauma in their earlier years that most of us don't just "get over" with the passage of time. If you *could* simply just "get over" it with the passage of time, senior citizens would be the happiest and mentally healthiest of all generations. In some cases, seeking therapy with a licensed professional is the best way to ensure that you and your relationship are on a sound footing and set up for success. An enlightened business would seek the assistance of an outside expert in a time of need, and your personal life is no different.

4) Intimacy—This category can be a challenge since, so often, intimacy is seen as another word for sex. In this dimension of the relationship discussion, sex is certainly something to talk about, given the potential differences in sexual appetites of men and women. However, for the sake of discussion, let's agree that there is a difference between sex and intimacy. It is not uncommon for spouses to have sexual contact without experiencing intimacy. While that is not necessarily bad on occasion, it will not be enough to sustain the relationship in the long term.

The key is to remember that true intimacy at the emotional level is what most partners want in their committed relationship, but they may not have a clue about how to achieve it. Just watch a few days of commercials or popular television sitcoms and you will see many examples of those simplistic, one-dimensional fantasy relationships mentioned in the introduction.

In such televised depictions, men are preoccupied with sex and see women as nothing but sex objects, while women are preoccupied with sex and see men as nothing but sex objects. In addition, these television shows often portray men as openly distasteful of anything that hints of emotional vulnerability, while women are often shown as lost, lonely, and emotionally desperate.

> *My wife Charlotte and I have a dinner/date night almost every other week. We take turns choosing a place and activity, and whoever is in charge brings two specific questions about deep and intimate issues that we want to discuss with each other but often don't take the time to, or may find risky. The evening usually ends up being insightful, interesting, fun, and physically intimate. A sampling of these questions is provided at the end of this chapter.*

In many of these sitcoms, women seem to be paired up with one of those simplistic, one-dimensional men who love themselves, their sports, their beer, or their car more than they love the desperate women who are constantly trying to trap, trick, or get rid of them. Is it any wonder that the popularity of marriage is at a 40-year low?

As I've mentioned before, having an intimate relationship is not about finding the right person; it is about being the right person. Intimacy is about having deep, loving feelings for your partner and being committed to meeting *that person's* needs and supporting *that person's* growth. Many women find intimacy in snuggling, deep conversations, having their partners show sincere interest in their lives, and receiving tokens of their partners' affection (a nice card, flowers, a dinner out). For many men, their partner's showing a genuine interest in their work, their ideas, and their ambitions often conveys intimacy.

5) Spirituality—This dimension is about what, if any, religious or spiritual beliefs are important to each of you and how you see religion being integrated with raising children. If you share the same religion and choose to practice it in the same manner, then this will likely be an easy and brief discussion. However, if there is a difference of opinion about religion or if a chasm exists, now is the time to bring it out and determine your objectives for this dimension of your relationship.

If neither of you is the "religious type," then, at a minimum, consider developing a set of core values that you want to live by... things like integrity, forgiveness, support, trust, compassion. Then develop a code of conduct that will define specific behaviors that reflect these values and how you will address behaviors that do not. This is the time to discuss consequences, what will happen if one partner behaves in a manner that does not reflect agreed upon values. If you jointly claim to value integrity but a partner has an affair, spell out what will be the consequence. Does it mean an immediate divorce, no questions asked? OR, if you also include forgiveness as a core value, does this mean that an affair, while being a complete violation of integrity and trust, may be forgiven depending on the circumstances and following lots of marriage counseling?

Just as in business, when insubordination or stealing from your employer means immediate termination, in *The Business of Love*, it is equally important to discuss consequences for breaking your shared religious morals or core values. This may seem cold or even harsh, but I would argue that this type of clarity would only help to strengthen the intimacy between partners. While much in an intimate relationship may be in shades of gray due to the need for ongoing negotiations and compromise, some things *are* black and white. As you can see, this dimension of your relationship is likely to bring out some strong reactions and powerful emotions, but don't avoid it since objectives in the spiritual dimension of your relationship will be used throughout other activities in this book and will be referenced later.

Unlike the days of marriages of means, when fathers determined everything for the couple, including what religion they would practice, these days people all too often marry with little concern about a lack of shared religious beliefs or common values. However, in the development of objectives for your relationship, please be thoughtful and deliberate, as your decisions in the spiritual dimension of your relationship will likely affect many, if not all, of the other dimensions. You may not be aware of the ways in which spirituality affects your life now, but that will likely change at some time in the future.

Most important, remember that religious beliefs and core values are not something you can compromise on without taking a toll on the relationship, and communication alone will rarely resolve a beliefs of values conflict.

6) Leisure—In this dimension, you may want to discuss when and how to travel, your hobbies, how to spend time off, your weekend activities, and the pace at which you want to live. Some people, like my wife, would rather have a slower, relaxed pace of life, while others, like me, prefer to be always going, doing, and planning for the next activity.

Are you both the kind of people who like to take two weeks of vacation and lie on the beach in the islands? Maybe a timeshare in Hawaii makes sense as one of your fiscal objectives. Or do you prefer the eco-tourist lifestyle, heading off to Machu Picchu, the ancient Inca city high in the Andes Mountains, one year, and off to the rainforests of Thailand the next? Or are you somewhere in between (or split) on how you like to spend your time off? This can often be another great area to negotiate and to practice the all-important skill of compromise.

Besides travel and weekend leisure, you may want to discuss hobbies. Do you like to sail, play golf, hunt, garden, or paint with watercolors? All of these things require a time commitment and might or might not include your partner.

This is also an opportunity to consider taking up new leisure activities. Perhaps you'd like to take golf lessons, since she is already an avid golfer, or cooking, since he does such a great job in the kitchen preparing meals for friends and family. Sometimes collaborating with your partner can spark new interests and hobbies.

7) **Career**—Are you happy with your current position? Is work something that you find extremely rewarding? Does it define who you are, or is it something you do just to pay

the bills? Many men are programmed to believe that their work defines their identity while women are programmed to believe that their family defines their identity. While each belief has its merits, each one also leaves you vulnerable to the cyclical and unpredictable nature of both work and family. You can begin to see why it is important to plan a lot of time to fully discuss each dimension so that you can define specific objectives that you both would like to accomplish. In your career discussions, be sure to detail how you see your career integrating with your family. For most dual-income couples, these are two sides of the same coin; balancing these often conflicting roles can be the source of chronic tension and anger. How to successfully achieve this balance will be discussed in more detail in Chapter 7 on job descriptions.

Some people's objectives may be to change careers altogether, while some may want to change their hours or to work from home. Discuss aspirations and dreams openly with each other and really listen to your partner.

8) Life-Long Learning—Are you interested in completing your nursing degree, getting an MBA, or being certified in scuba diving? Reasons to gain more formal or informal education and training can include furthering your career (if so, don't forget to mention this in the career dimension) or just because it will make you happy. You might have dreams of going to cooking school in France so you can someday open your own restaurant. Perhaps the ambition underlying your desire to learn to sew is to develop a unique line of clothing that you can sell on eBay. If you yearn to develop a new craft or skill that requires further education, it will fall under this dimension.

> *"In a time of drastic change it is the learners who inherit the future. The learned usually find themselves equipped to live in a world that no longer exists."*—Eric Hoffer, writer, philosopher and longshoreman.

In the business world, organizations committed to learning, evolving and adapting to changing circumstances consistently outperform those who do not. In addition, the mentally healthiest among us are those individuals and couples committed to learning, evolving and adapting to changing circumstances.

Therefore, if I had to prioritize these dimensions, I would put life-long learning as one of the most important. Each of us, to be most effective in all dimensions of our lives, must consider learning as part of a birth-to-death process. Broadly defined, life-long learning is based on the principle that it is never too early or too late to learn and that education can be flexible, diverse and accessed at different times and places throughout our lifecycle. Life-Long Learning includes:

1. **Learning to know**—acquiring information and knowledge to expand your consciousness about the world in which you live. In light of the other dimensions detailed in this chapter,

this might include deepening your religious beliefs, understanding your emotional intelligence, or enhancing your mental health.

2. **Learning to do**—acquiring skills and abilities to produce results, perform tasks and achieve specific outcomes. This includes completing a college degree, learning how to raise an autistic child, or learning how to start your own business.

3. **Learning to be**—acquiring the skills and abilities needed to build and sustain productive relationships. This could include supervisory training to better manage employees, relationship-enrichment training to improve communication skills, or diversity training to overcome your ethnic prejudices.

Regardless of what you decide to learn and how you decide to do it, life-long learning can be one key to success in each aspect and at every stage of your life. Life-Long Learning is what this book is all about.

Set clear objectives

When discussing each life dimension, take time to set clear objectives for what you would like to accomplish, fully hear each other out, and then come up with outcomes that work for you both. If you identify other dimensions that are important to you and your partner, feel free to add them to your list. These objectives, grouped into the various dimensions, are provided only as examples. You may find that several of the dimensions and the objectives listed within them work for you with little or no editing. Or you may find that you need to develop a completely different set of your own dimensions and objectives. Now it is time for your detailed work to begin. It is okay to develop many drafts, change the wording, and do lots of editing... just get started, but be sure to use a pencil with a good eraser or be prepared to make many changes in the objectives on your computer. *Dimensions and objective setting worksheets are available in the Workbook that accompanies this book that can be found at www.thebusinessoflove.org*

SAMPLE DIMENSIONS & OBJECTIVES WORKSHEET

Dimensions:	*Objectives:*	
1. Family	1.1	Have a family meal at the dining room table at least 3 times weekly.
	1.2	Limit television watching to only those programs we select in advance.
	1.3	Develop a relationship with at least one culturally diverse family a year.
	1.4	Avoid racist, religiously biased or gender-stereotypical comments ever.
	1.5	Begin discussing assisted-living options for our mother with my sisters before the end of the year.
	1.6	Get a small-breed dog in the next 2 years.
	1.7	Decide whether to have, or to adopt, children in the next 3 years.

2. Fiscal	2.1 Consolidate our investments into one brokerage account within the next 6 months.
	2.2 Complete a will with a living trust by the end of the year.
	2.3 Re-evaluate the amount of life insurance for each of us and adjust accordingly every 3 years.
	2.4 Donate 5% of our net income on an annualized basis.
	2.5 Develop a cash rainy-day fund equal to 3 months of living expenses within the next 3 years.
	2.6 Begin a 529 College Savings Plan for each child by the time they turn 3.
	2.7 Select a fee-only financial planner by the end of the year.
	2.8 Refinance our home to a fixed rate mortgage within 2 years.
	2.9 Diversify the 401(K) offered at work.
	2.10 Complete a detailed financial plan for the relationship by the end of this year and update it at least every 3 years.
3. Health & Wellness	3.1 Learn Hatha Yoga by the end of this year.
	3.2 Walk together for at least 30 minutes twice weekly.
	3.3 Get a complete physical by the end of the year.
	3.4 Reduce caffeine consumption to 2 cups of coffee—only in the morning.
	3.5 Begin strength training at the gym within 6 months.
	3.6 Attend a smoking-cessation class by the end of this year.

4. Intimacy	4.1	Go out on a "date" at least 2 times each month.
	4.2	Commit to not going to sleep before discussing something that might be troubling us.
	4.3	Do something romantic and unexpected at least once monthly.
	4.4	Learn how to give a massage to each other by our 10th anniversary.
	4.5	Read a relationship article or book together at least twice a year.
	4.6	Alternate who initiates sexual relations.
5. Spirituality	5.1	Find a new congregation within 5 miles of our new home by the end of the year.
	5.2	Visit the Holy Lands before our 1st child is born.
	5.3	Volunteer for a mission to Central America in the next 5 years.
	5.4	Read the Bible weekly.
	5.5	Attend religious services at least 2 times monthly.
6. Leisure	6.1	Take a family vacation at least twice a year.
	6.2	Take one international vacation at least once every 3 years.
	6.3	Vacation alone once every 10 years.
	6.4	Continue my coin collection and attend 2 collector shows a year.
	6.5	Begin planning a family reunion before Dad turns 80.
	6.6	Take dance lessons within 12 months.
	6.7	Learn to play the piano by my 50th birthday.

7. Career	7.1	Become department director by the time I reach 40.
	7.2	Accept a relocation offer only if we both agree it is best for us.
	7.3	Complete a retirement plan for Susan by the end of the year.
	7.4	Have our department adopt a school to support within 18 months.
	7.5	Become the leading region in sales within 18 months.
	7.6	Confer with George about my career options if I do not relocate.
8. Life-Long Learning:	8.1	Complete an MBA from an accredited university by the time I reach 35.
	8.2	Read at least 1 career-related book a month.
	8.3	Become proficient with one new software application every 6 months.
	8.4	Attend a parent-education class before our oldest child turns 3.
	8.5	Complete some type of relationship enrichment activity at least once every 3 years.

If you are a fan of developing lists and doing lots of detailed planning, you can drill down even deeper on your own with each objective. Consider the following as an example of the level of detail that might be helpful for you and your partner to ensure that you achieve what you set out to accomplish. It can feel very satisfying to come up with such a detailed roadmap to certain dimensions of your life and then actually achieving your objective. Look at one of your objectives in detail, as this example shows:

Dimensions and objective setting worksheets are available in the Workbook that accompanies this book that can be found at www.thebusinessoflove.org

Objective 8.1 – Complete an MBA from an accredited university by the time I reach 35.			
Action Step	*Interim completion date*	*Time/ Resources*	*Outcome/ Results*
8.1.1 – Apply for the GRE exam	April 10	3 hrs.	accepted
8.1.2 – Apply for tuition supplement from employer	May 25	2 hrs.	approval
8.1.3 – Research top 5 MBA programs in the region	May - July	12 hrs.	prioritized list
8.1.4 – Request undergraduate transcripts	June 15	1 hr.	receive
8.1.5 – Prepare for the GRE	July – Aug.	30-50 hrs.	1200+ score
8.1.6 – Apply to top 2 MBA programs	Aug. – Oct.	10-25 hrs.	submission
8.1.7 – Research and determine tuition budget	June – Aug.	5-10 hrs.	file
8.1.8 – Visit each campus	Oct. – Dec.	3 days	select program
8.1.9 – Prepare for enrollment	Jan. or Sept.	1 day	begin classes

By now, you might have built a good basis for the philosophical foundation of your relationship by completing a joint vision statement (it is okay if you have tabled the vision statement activity until later). However, if nothing else, you might now have a good start on developing a detailed set of S.M.A.R.T. objectives in each of the relationship dimensions.

You are almost ready to move on to the next step necessary to fulfill your relationship's vision and objectives... writing a job description for each partner to determine who will be responsible for each objective in every dimension. For example, if you've identified a number of financial objectives, you will need to decide who will manage the checking account, maintain the financial software, and conduct on-line banking, who will take the lead on filing taxes, who will make the investment decisions, and who will monitor the finances to make sure they are meeting your stated objectives. In addition, you need to decide how you will make major financial decisions like buying a home or automobile. Your job descriptions will need to answer these questions.

Before you move on to writing job descriptions on the tactical side of *The Business of Love* model, there are other prerequisite strategic topics that you need to address in the next chapters on funding the relationship, creating a "brand" image for your relationship and dealing with mergers and acquisitions.

However, before moving on, as I mentioned above, the

following is a list of some questions that my wife and I discuss during our dinner/date nights. First, give them some thought and write down or think about your answers. Then, maybe you'll want to discuss one, two, or all of your answers with your partner. Whether responses to these questions are kept private or shared, these questions are good "food for thought" and typically increase emotional intimacy.

Twenty questions to build intimacy!

1. What is your favorite term of endearment (honey, sweetie, etc.)?
2. What do you like most about my kissing? Least?
3. When you pray, what do you pray for?
4. What is your biggest fear about asserting yourself with me? With others?
5. What is one habit I have that you wish I would change?
6. What would you like to be doing when you are 40, 60, or 80?
7. Do you think God has a physical form? If so, what is it?
8. Do you swear when you are not around me; if so, what causes you to do it?
9. Do you ever think about divorcing me? What would cause you to take that action?
10. Do you fear that I would ever leave you? For what reason?
11. Do you ever think that our marriage was a mistake?
12. What are you most proud of in our marriage?
13. What is one material possession you do not have but wish you did?

14. What do you think happens when we die?

15. What scares you most about your marriage to me?

16. Have you ever thought about having an affair during our marriage?

17. What is your biggest financial worry?

18. Where is your favorite place to make love?

19. When is your favorite time of day?

20. What do you fear most about being more emotionally intimate with me?

Chapter Highlights:

- *Discussing your shared desires and priorities as a couple*

- *Deciding what life dimensions best fit your life together*

- *Creating a shared set of S.M.A.R.T. objectives that work in conjunction with your vision statement*

STRATEGIC: *Relating to the identification of long-term aims and interests, and the means of achieving them!*

Chapter 4—Funding the Partnership Venture— Best Practice #3

"Disposable income is a good thing."
—Richard Bloodworth, my very best friend

Chapter Objectives:

1. Determine your attitudes about money and how it affects your relationship.

2. Understand how your history with money affects your own as well as your partner's financial objectives as adults.

3. Discuss ways to negotiate, compromise or change things for the better when it comes to dealing with money in your relationship.

Dear John,

I have a classic marital problem for you. My wife and I have been married for 17 years and have always argued about money. She wants to save every dime for some rainy day in the future and I want to spend it on a great life today. In these days and times, I'm not sure if I'll ever be able to fully retire from work and have that free time to do as I please.

I want to travel and do things outside of work while I'm young and energetic (I'm in my mid-40s). My wife wants to plan for a retirement where we can do all the things we want after our kids are grown. We agree on many other issues, but not on money. How can we bridge the money gap?

Signed,
Separated by Money
Ashland, OR

Money might not buy happiness, but it can sure expand your range of choices while waiting for happiness to arrive. In addition, it can, unfortunately, increase the likelihood of conflicts over how to spend "disposable income," which is the money left over for our wants after we pay for our needs. Few things in our lives bring out stronger emotional reactions than how we feel about money and, as you know, a couple may have very different attitudes about it. The way we handle money and our view of its role in a relationship usually comes from the way we were raised and how our parents dealt with money. Don't worry, "Separated by Money," it just takes some understanding, negotiations and compromise, as you'll see in this chapter.

How *do* you feel about money?

As I mentioned in the Introduction, conflicts about money, children and household chores are the top sources of relationship conflict. Since money is such a significant problem in relationships, I feel it needs greater emphasis.

But before we go any further, here's my disclaimer. This chapter is not about investments, retirement planning, the best income tax software, or which financial advisor to choose. Instead, this chapter is about funding the vision for your relationship, ensuring the resources are there to achieve your objectives, and discovering your attitudes that affect how each of you deals with money.

In a business environment, it is often easy to see what motivates a company. Money is either a means or an end. Simply stated, some companies focus on providing superior quality products and services and taking care of their employees and their customers, expecting the profits will come. Companies that focus on (and are known for) superior products and services consistently, over the long-term, outperform those who do not. The company's focus is on sustainability, and its leaders concentrate on leaving a legacy.

Other companies' leaders are driven by profit alone, and make decisions based on the prospect of short-term financial gains without concern about the company in the long term. This may not be as bad as it sounds, since our current dynamic economic environment might dictate a short-term focus of getting in there, making some money, and getting out fast before technology changes, competition overwhelms you, or the whims of customers change.

Unfortunately, if you and your partner have differing attitudes toward money as a means or an end (as in the letter from "Separated By Money" above), you will need to have some clarifying conversations in search of common ground in funding your relationship enterprise. Differences over money are not something that you can simply agree to disagree on.

First, it's important to understand how you feel about money. Is it something you hoard and fear spending, or do you spend every cent you make, or are you somewhere in between? What is your relationship with money? Historically, what attitudes toward money and wealth did you grow up with, and do you still feel this way now? Do you believe that the man should make more money than the woman and, if so, why? Do you connect your self-worth to the size of your paycheck?

After you figure out how you feel about money, listen to what your partner has to say about money, too. Be honest and talk about it with each other. If you've never thought about it before, you may be amazed at what you can learn about yourself and your partner.

Family myths

It is also helpful to think about your parents' attitudes and how these attitudes affected their marriage. You'll most likely find a pattern there for why you feel a certain way toward money and all that it can symbolize. In fact, I'm sure if you looked at how their parents (your grandparents) handled money, you'd find a similar pattern there, too.

For example, my wife Charlotte grew up in a household where no one talked about money, though the family was financially well-off. Her father supplemented spending time with her and her siblings by spending money on them. For Charlotte's family, money was secretive and something that the man of the house was expected to handle. Her father often gave her money while simultaneously saying, "Do you think money grows on trees?" She knew he worked hard for the family's income but she had no concept of money and wealth management. So, you can imagine how surprised she was when I asked her to take over the management of our personal checking account and bookkeeping software. She now manages the checkbook using financial software, routinely making electronic fund transfers and paying bills online. Since she spends 90% of the money in the household, it is logical for her to manage it on a day-to-day basis. She gets to see how much money comes in and how much money goes out. Her relationship to money has completely transformed her attitudes about it, as well as changed the face of what our partnership means to her. She used to think that it was rude to ask about money, and I assumed that she did not care about family finances. Now, however, money is no longer a secretive topic or a substitute for something else. It simply sustains our lifestyle. She manages money in an efficient and frugal manner and is a great bargain shopper, and I never worry about her wasting or mismanaging our joint incomes.

As for me, I grew up in a home where there never seemed to be enough money. The subject of money and its absence in my family brought about feelings of anxiety. My father did not bring in a steady income. My mother's job sustained us, but we all knew that things were tight.

I was the kind of kid who saved every penny. I even made money by digging through dumpsters at the local bike shop for spare parts to make bicycles. I sold them to the kids in the neighborhood for $5, but rarely spent a penny of it. As an adult, I am still frugal, yet I've learned to overcome many of those early uncomfortable feelings about money through a faith-based money management class. This class gave me a new sense of peace about money and material goods and the proper stewardship of both.

Dealing with our attitudes

We also get our attitudes from various places other than family, such as education, media, peers, society and, in particular, religion. Often religion and wealth are seen as opposites, and certain uninformed zealots like to tell us "money is the root of all evil." For the sake of this discussion about money, religion and funding your marital vision, it is important to note that the actual verse is, "The *love* of money is the root of all evil." (1 Timothy 6:10) Big difference! Having

68

money and enjoying your life does not necessarily lead to evil or sin—only a greedy, unnatural focus on money and materialism leads there. God never expected people to be broke! Love your partner, not your money.

Many of us in a long-term relationship will have psychological issues to work out with regard to money so that it won't hurt our relationship. Use the questions at the end of this chapter to help identify your attitudes about money. Share your thoughts on the differences and/or similarities in your attitudes about money, material goods and wealth management. Is it a means or an end in your life?

Many dual-income couples struggle with priorities and get caught in the trap of "needing" the two incomes because it buys them the lifestyle they think makes them happy or that they feel pressured to create. But this may backfire, since the couple ends up resenting work because they spend so much time apart trying to earn the money to be able to enjoy time together… get the paradox? The one thing the couple wants to do is to have a good life and share time together—yet they are robbed of it because they are in the dual-income trap. More money, obviously, doesn't always make for more happiness.

From my perspective, money buys choices and freedom from certain burdens—nothing more. In the pressure of a business or intimate relationship, money often becomes the focus of the power struggles I mentioned earlier in this chapter. When there's a financial power struggle, money becomes a tool for manipulation—warped into something more than it is.

THE BUSINESS OF LOVE

Understand where you and your partner's attitudes about money come from and discuss ways to negotiate, compromise or change things for the better. To be in an intimate relationship, yet not fight about money is such a glorious luxury in today's society. Be on the cutting edge and work to free your relationship of one of the most common power struggles that can damage or destroy even the most loving relationship! In *The Business of Love*, financial serenity is possible with your *current* income... it's just that you both might have some background work to do in order to actually believe that and truly feel that way.

Money & Attitudes Questions
1. What role did money play in your life as a child?
2. How did your parents feel about money?
3. How did your parents' attitudes about money affect you?
4. Have you or someone you've known ever used money to manipulate or dominate? Why? What was the result?
5. What role does money play in your life now?
6. How much is your self-concept tied to your income?
7. What do you or will you teach your children about money?
8. Have you ever spent money to avoid or overcome an emotionally upsetting situation? When? What was the outcome?
9. Do you think men should make more money than women and why?
10. Should we share one bank account or keep them separate?

A relationship, money and attitudes worksheet is available in the Workbook that accompanies this book that can be found at www.thebusinessoflove.org

Chapter Highlights:

- *Understanding how you feel about money and how it affects your relationship*
- *Looking at how your upbringing and your family's attitudes about money plays into your own attitudes about it*
- *Negotiating and compromising with your partner to ensure that you share productive attitudes about money as you fund your relationship vision and work to achieve your common objectives*

STRATEGIC: *Relating to the identification of long-term aims and interests, and the means of achieving them!*

Chapter 5—Branding and Marketing Your Relationship— Best Practice #4

"You can't blow an uncertain trumpet."—Fr. Theodore Hesburgh, former President, University of Notre Dame

Chapter Objectives:

1. Learn what a relationship brand is and why it is important.
2. Have fun finding the brand logo or symbol that you both can agree on.
3. Discover how and why to market your relationship brand to family and friends.

Dear John,

I've been married for 11 years to my wonderful wife and mother of our five children. I am very proud of our abilities to balance both the work and family issues that come with having a dual-income family. What distresses me is that when we get together with our friends, I hear my wife tell her friends I don't do enough around the house and that I am always traveling. My job does require me to travel fairly often (though I got her approval to take this job knowing that fact) and I do all the handyman stuff around the house and even a few errands for the kids when I'm not working.

While I probably don't do as much as some dads/husbands who have job flexibility, I feel like the things I do are appreciated by my wife. But in public, she jokingly bad-mouths me to her friends. As you can imagine, this makes me feel badly about our relationship. What can I do to get her to stop publicly criticizing me and speak more favorably about us?

Signed,
The Stereotyped Husband
Bangor, Maine

Who "we" are!

Relationships have two faces: a private one and a public one. It is not uncommon for those faces to be different and even divisive, but it is unfortunate. The bigger the gap between the two faces, the bigger the risks to the long-term sustainability of the relationship. While there are certain aspects of any relationship that are best kept private, it is critical that both the internal and external faces of the relationship be based on a common vision and objectives that collectively identify the relationship "brand."

The biggest benefit of branding and marketing your relationship is that it ensures that whenever you or your partner describe the relationship to others, you are both drawing from the same vision, values and attitudes about the relationship. This strengthens the psychological bond, fortifies the emotional commitment and adds to the level of intimacy each of you feels toward the other.

The problem occurs when couples are not unified in their relationship "brand," so that they seem to be describing two very different relationships. In this chapter, we will discuss developing a unified "brand" for your relationship and the importance of consistently marketing it to your family and friends.

A critical element for success in any business is for it to have a very clear sense of its identity—what it stands for, the emotional relationship it hopes to establish with its customers—and an ability to market that sense of identity to the world. This means going beyond the company's vision and objectives to formulate a brand that fits the business philosophically and typically conjures up an emotional response and connection for the customer.

Nike, Coke, Apple, Mercedes and Harley-Davidson are

some of the most recognized brands in the world. When you see any of these company logos, they cause an immediate emotional response and, whether your reaction is positive or negative, you feel it right away. You get a clear sense of what Mercedes and Apple stand for from the marketing of those logos and the concepts of who they are as a company. A brand is simply a symbol of that identity—a reminder of your emotional relationship with the company behind the logo.

An example from my consulting work with a law firm provides insight into the role and significance of relationship branding. A colleague and I were helping a law firm build a strategic plan that included a marketing program. These were personal injury lawyers who had a hard time breaking out of the stereotypical image of ambulance chasers. My colleague was a brand specialist, and he gave the partners of the firm an assignment using magazines and newspapers, scissors, some glue, and poster board. He told them to cut out the images that portrayed what they did not want to be, as well as the images of what they did want to be as a firm. It ended up being a fascinating exercise for them. They took those "anti-images" (an ad with an overweight guy in a Hawaiian shirt holding a martini and smoking a big cigar, and surrounded by voluptuous women in bikinis around a hotel pool in Las Vegas) and glued them onto one big piece of poster board.

On the other poster board was, among other more positive images, a picture of a lion's head with a strong and confident look on its face, which the partners saw as reflecting integrity and the courage to do battle if need be. That lion's head ended up as a symbol of their brand, and it became the logo for the firm. The firm uses these poster board images of what they do and do not want to be to make sure they are still on the right path. That is an example of a brand logo: a symbol that conjures up emotions, values or beliefs of what you stand for and want others to know about your brand.

Branding a relationship means that you both work to find a symbol, a logo, that represents what you, the partners, see as the essence of your relationship. As you might have guessed, I'm going to ask you to do the same exercise as the attorneys in the law firm. Make it a fun event some evening, and while it may seem silly at first, it can be a powerful way to create a brand logo of who you are as a couple. Work together to go through magazines, newspapers or the Internet to collect images of what your relationship is and what it is not.

Try to agree on one or two images that may work in unison with each other. If you really do not agree on an image, take more time to discuss it. Or, if you find nothing in any of these sources, maybe one of you could design a new image encompassing both of your ideas. It can even be a newly created symbol, but just make sure that the symbol gives both of you a sense of meaning and reminds you of the essence of your relationship whenever you see it. In addition, even consider identifying a song that supports your brand and will further identify your relationship. Intel, the giant computer microchip maker, has done a great job of linking a familiar four-part tone in all their commercials to their brand. Anytime we hear the familiar tone in a commercial, most of us will immediately think of Intel. Beethoven's Ode to Joy was played at our wedding, and our son and daughter-in-law had it played for us, as we walked down the aisle, at their wedding. Whenever Charlotte or I hear that music, we have a rush of warm emotions.

Keep the poster boards, unified symbol, or a version of the song so you can revisit these images at your annual retreat (see Chapter 10 on Meetings & Retreats), and make sure that you, too, use your brand to stay on the path to a world-class relationship.

Marketing your relationship's brand

So, you've found or created a brand logo that represents who you are as a couple. Now, it is time to let others know what your relationship is all about. In the business world, it is about marketing your brand. But why do you need to market something so intimate to the people in your lives, you ask? First, let's take a brief look at why businesses market their brand images.

Companies typically market to sell more products and services. In addition, companies market their brand for other reasons: they market to keep loyal customers, to stay ahead of their competition, to sell more to existing customers, to attract employees and even to attract other organizations who want to work in partnership with them. In other words, companies need stakeholders, partners and friends who believe in what they do and who want to associate with them.

In a relationship, while you have each other, it is also normal and healthy to spend time with family and friends. Even though you clearly have no product or service to sell, one key benefit of developing and marketing your marital brand is that you are likely to attract other like-minded couples. This both reinforces the relationship that you have and helps you to learn from the relationships of others by "benchmarking" your relationship with those around you.

This simply means that you use the relationships of others as a point of reference to determine the health of your relationship. It is hard enough to find good examples of positive and productive relationships anywhere in our society. So anytime that you can learn the "best practices" of other healthy couples through comparative benchmarking, you enhance the return on your investment in developing and marketing your relationship brand.

If you and your partner are ever in a social situation with other couples and you find yourself uncomfortable with the nature of the interactions and behavior of other couples, be sure to discuss your emotional reaction later in private. It is not that you will gossip about or judge others; instead, it is an excellent opportunity to do comparative benchmarking by recognizing what you do or don't want in your relationship. On the other hand, perhaps you may feel a bit envious because you see something modeled by another couple that you would like to have more of in your relationship. Be sure to talk about it as well and consider it a great opportunity to learn how to strengthen your relationship by learning from the best practices modeled by other couples.

There's another reason to do relationship brand marketing. It is my belief that if you don't give people a positive perception of who you are as a couple, they will make one up for themselves and categorize you in a way that might be negative and/or unwanted. As mentioned, all relationships have different faces, and people see only the face that you show them. Sometimes the opinions others form about you as a couple can be harmful to your relationship.

Take, for example, the stereotypical situation with the in-laws. Do you ever go to dinner with your or your partner's parents, and one of them takes your partner's side on every issue? Or worse, they pick on your partner and never give him or her any support? Why is that? It is possibly because the parents don't see you as a cohesive couple with a united front. In fact, these episodes with the parents may cause you to fight all the way home, becoming exactly as the in-laws see you: divided against each other. It can be a self-fulfilling prophecy when people emphasize a certain image of you, and that certainly holds true for a couple, too. If your friends take you and your partner's playful banter as true fighting, they may egg you on at every gathering or party, which can escalate to real arguments that in time may start to weaken your relationship.

Purposely marketing a unified brand of who you are as a couple will let the people you spend time with know the brand of your relationship and how you want to be viewed. Now, this doesn't mean that you can't be yourselves and continue that playful banter. But once in awhile, one of you can say something like, "One thing I love about Gina is that she likes to tease me as much as I love to tease her. We are both very playful that way."

I'm not suggesting you and your partner be people you are not. It's quite the opposite. I am asking you to *know* who you are as a couple—your brand—and to market it appropriately as a key strategy toward continually strengthening your relationship. Nike, Coke and McDonalds continually market their brands to reinforce the image of who they are and what they stand for. In *The Business of Love*, you and your partner continually market your brand to ensure those around you know what you stand for as a couple.

The united front

Parents often talk about the importance of presenting a united front when dealing with their children. Of course, this doesn't mean you are clones of one another, but it does mean you both set the rules and enforce them with similar, agreed-upon methods. If parents don't form a united front, the kids may see the differences as vulnerabilities and use them against the parents. It's no different with friends and family.

Pick out those qualities or values from your brand that you most want to put forth. No matter what your wife says to other people about you, always make sure that they know she supports you. No matter what your husband forgets to do or how frustrated you or others can get with him, let them know you are with him all the way. While venting your irritation about your partner to a close friend, it's a good idea to add, something like "Oh well, it's a good thing we share the same vision and values, it helps me get past the occasional little disagreements quickly." Live the brand!

In business, it's sometimes mentioned that you should have an "elevator speech" for what you do—meaning a quick description of what you do for a living that you can give in just a few moments. When you meet someone on an elevator who says, "What do you do for XYZ Corporation?" it's good to have a well-thought-out and crisp answer ready. The same goes for your relationship. When someone asks, "So you've been together for 9 years now, huh? Wow," or "I heard you got remarried. How's it going?" It's good to have a genuine answer that reaffirms your feelings about the relationship, "I've found my best friend and married him and we just keep getting better every day!" It is like having a tag line for your relationship just like the corporate brands.

As a counterbalance to the chronically high divorce rate, consider becoming much more purposeful in the care and nurturing of the most important relationship in your life. Discovering or developing your authentic relationship brand and marketing it consistently can be a powerful tool to help keep you both well connected... and make the relationship world-class.

This is a chance for you to feel more in charge of your relationship's destiny. To take relationship brand marketing one step further, consider creating your own website since it is so easy to do. It's the place where you post pictures or notices of your partnership or family events and market your brand to the world. Write quarterly e-newsletters to all of your family and friends that reinforce the brand images of who you are as a couple. Building a world-class relationship means you need to do things differently to make your relationship successful. Developing and marketing a relationship brand is certainly outside-the-box thinking!

Chapter Highlights:

- *Understanding what a relationship brand is, why you need one and how to live the brand*
- *Identifying and agreeing on your specific relationship brand image, symbol, or song*
- *Using the brand to market who you are as a couple to your family and friends*

STRATEGIC: Relating to the identification of long-term aims and interests, and the means of achieving them!

Chapter 6—Growing the Relationship: Mergers and Acquisitions— Best Practice #5

"Growth is the only evidence of life."
—Cardinal John Henry Newman

Chapter Objectives:

1. Explore the significant differences between what it means to be a family today compared to a family in the past.

2. Understand mergers and acquisitions in the context of couples and families.

3. Blend family and life cultures based on differing family histories.

4. Learn how to deal with the consequences of marrying into a blended family situation without losing your identity or uniqueness for the sake of the relationship.

Dear John,

I am a 22-year-old devout Roman Catholic woman who has fallen in love with a 28-year- old Jewish man with two young kids from a previous marriage. He is very close to these kids and seems to be a great father. He is also a kind and gentle person who loves me, too. We want to get married, but I can't stop wondering how we can handle all the complexity that our relationship has from the very start. Not only are we different religiously (which seems to be a bigger deal to me than him), but also I'd be a stepmother at such a young age. Any advice at all would be appreciated!

Signed,
No Experience Stepmother
Springfield, IL

Well, No Experience Stepmother, you do have a significant challenge ahead of you. But if you are diligent before your marital merger and the acquisition of stepchildren takes place, you may find that the challenge will be less troublesome and even enlightening. Read on for more information

86

on the kind of relationship you are entering and how to avoid the pitfalls and to ensure that everyone gains in the new enterprise.

Looking for growth opportunities

The hyper-competitive, survival of the fittest business environment that we have today means there are only two options: growth or extinction. One of the prime ways a business grows in today's dynamic marketplace is through mergers and acquisitions. Businesses may merge with or buy other companies to expand the scope of their core products and services, to diversify into new markets, or to completely reinvent who they are. Why take the time to develop new products and services when you can simply buy an established and successful business that is already providing them?

Today's families must also cope in a very dynamic environment where the traditional family with a male breadwinner, female homemaker and 3.2 children is rare and certainly no longer considered "traditional." The definition of what it means to be a family has undergone a permanent transformation from a monolithic image to a mosaic of differing pieces. Families today are often complex, as more and more people marry into blended families, people of different races and religions join together, and aging parents move in with their grown children. The blended family has become the norm and accounts for 60% of all families, and, to be successful, this new type of family may need some new strategies to blend "yours, mine and ours!" Families no longer grow simply by conceiving more children; rather, much like a business, they also grow through mergers and acquisitions.

To merge or acquire?

Typically, when two companies merge, the hope is that the whole will be greater than the sum of the parts. Ideally, two businesses uniting actually work to create a whole new organization with a fresh identity and culture. This hoped for "new identity" is an idealized state that is also the goal when getting married. Healthy relationships mean creating a new partnership that allows each participant to gain, grow and benefit; in other words, to profit from the union by bringing together two entities to form a more valuable and worthy enterprise.

In the context of *The Business of Love*, a marital merger is based on an equal pairing of partners who have decided to move from a "sole proprietorship" to form a new entity (the couple) with no children or other family. On the other hand, a marital acquisition takes place when you commit to a relationship where you acquire more than just a spouse. You also gain a larger enterprise that might include stepchildren or live-in parents. Beyond this, you are gaining in-laws who, for better or worse, come as part of the deal.

To give you an example, let's take a page out of my personal history. Charlotte and I are both married for the second time. In my first marriage, (which was a merger) neither of us had been married previously and we did not bring children into the marriage. However, in my marriage to Charlotte,

I purposely looked for a woman who already had children so I could also be a father. More specifically, I was in my 40s and did not want to father children, but I sure wanted to experience parenting by being a good stepfather with a partner who already had children. So, for women who think that being a single mom is a liability, I can tell you confidently that I've known a number of men who have actively searched for a woman with kids, to acquire a "ready-made" family.

My choice to marry Charlotte meant that I immediately acquired new responsibilities as a stepparent as well, and now as a grandfather. It was not all smooth sailing in the beginning, since we all had to make adjustments and compromises. Now, however, my stepson and stepdaughter actually call me their "extra father" rather than their stepfather. While their natural father is still very much a positive part of their lives, the term "extra father" means that, for them, I am more significant to their lives than what is implied by the mundane term, "step-father." I enjoy my relationship with them immensely, love them more than I can ever show, and feel fortunate to be a part of their lives and have them as a part of mine!

In addition, you've likely known others who merged with partners with children and they went on to grow their "enterprise" by giving birth to new children.

The challenges of mergers and acquisitions

As an organizational development consultant, I am sometimes hired to help manage the change that occurs during the transition that results from a merger or acquisition. In a lot of ways, this work is similar to what I did as a marriage counselor years ago when couples were remarrying. As a counselor then and as a consultant now, my job is to help successfully blend the previously separate and sometimes quite different (corporate or family) cultures into a new enterprise that achieves what both parties envisioned when they decided to join forces.

When dealing with a merger or acquisition, there are two essential dimensions in a business that need to be considered. The first element is the structural dimension, which includes the physical elements of the business, systems, processes, organizational structure, workforce, facilities, inventory, and so on. During most mergers and acquisitions, the focus is on the structural dimension—deciding which plants to close, what HR system is the most effective, consolidating warehouse operations, laying off staff, and so on. What gets missed is the cultural dimension, which is far more important for success and involves the less visible, yet very powerful, aspects of operations, such as the patterns of communication, company values, levels of teamwork, organizational history, workload, attitudes of workers, history of change, and so on. As consultants, we go in and research the different cultures by conducting staff interviews, surveys and focus groups to determine what the cultures are like and what the organizations' "change readiness" capabilities are.

A business merger or acquisition is a challenging undertaking, and unfortunately, in many cases, the whole becomes less than the sum of the parts if both the structural and cultural dimensions are not proactively addressed. The same can be said of an intimate relationship. It can be a very difficult process integrating families and backgrounds, and the fact that second marriages do not last as long as first marriages, and the divorce rates for second marriages exceed those for first marriages, bears out this point.

Essentially, you'll need to integrate the structural components of what both parties bring to the relationship, such as financial assets, homes, automobiles, furniture, and other possessions. But you also have to integrate the cultural dimension, such as visions, objectives and values that each of you brings to the relationship. Beyond these key strategic factors, you will need to successfully integrate patterns of communication, negotiation styles, problem solving skills, and stress-coping mechanisms. If you did not already include learning new interpersonal skills to strengthen your relationship while developing your objectives, consider going back to the objective setting activity in Chapter 3. Review your Life-Long Learning dimension and consider adding education about blended families and step-parenting as a key objective that you want to accomplish, as soon as possible.

Suppose for a moment that you fall in love with a woman who has two sons and an aging, senile mother who lives with them. Do you run away screaming, "It can't be done," which is certainly a viable option, or do you roll up your sleeves and accept the challenge of a very tough acquisition? Remember that nothing worthwhile is ever easy.

Conversely, trying to combine a secular Jew with a devout Catholic (as in the letter at the beginning of the chapter) can be a recipe for a disastrous merger if the culture issues are not dealt with head on.

Blending family cultures

Cul•ture, *n.*: *"The beliefs, customs, practices and behavior of the individuals whose shared experiences identify the particular relationship of which they are a part; a particular set of attitudes and behaviors that characterizes the relationship."*

The most common form of a blended family appears when a couple remarries and is raising children from previous relationships. Nationally, nearly 60% of all families have children from other parents or from different marriages. Parenting in a blended family is not necessarily more difficult than parenting in general, but it can include some very unique challenges.

The potential conflicts that might arise between partners with regard to parenting are likely to be values conflicts over things like disciplining children or needs conflicts over things like children's bedtime. As described in the discussion on negotiation, value conflicts are much more difficult to address and are rarely resolved by compromising on your standards of discipline, while a conflict of needs over bedtime, for example, may be easy to resolve through compromise. The key to successfully blending family cultures, in the context of *The Business of Love*, is to ensure that you and your partner establish a common vision that includes the children, establish clear objectives regarding how the children will be raised, and determine your parenting roles and responsibilities as part of writing your job descriptions.

Gaining a partner, not losing yourself

No one purposely enters a relationship to lose "who *they* are." Neither you nor your partner wants to lose your respective personal identities, beliefs or values when you marry. A remarriage resulting in a blended family means roles will change, priorities may shift and parental attention may be diverted to the new spouse. The overarching goal here is to keep the best of each person's personal "life culture." That's why many of the exercises in this book are meant to help you strengthen who you are as an individual while eliminating barriers in your relationship by discussing, not avoiding, difficult issues. Growing your relationship, like growing a business, takes forethought and courage to focus on and resolve what is most contentious, so that the love and intimacy can flourish with fewer roadblocks.

So how do you measure beliefs, customs, practices and behavior that are vague? One example comes from a current client of mine who is rolling out a new values initiative within her company. She hopes this plan will result in higher levels of employee commitment through values-driven recruiting, hiring, orientation, performance management and compensation. The company wants to create a culture that is open and creative, so employees can do their very best. We've been planning the big kickoff meeting for this initiative, involving their frontline employees meeting with senior management. One of the planners within the company gasped at the thought of frontline employees being asked to talk candidly about ways to improve operations with their bosses in the room. My reply was to remind her that this inability to talk openly within the current corporate culture is exactly what this initiative is aiming to reverse. So you can see why, during times of corporate mergers, it is much easier to talk about closing plants and laying off workers than how to enhance employee performance and team effectiveness.

In a relationship, it is often easy to identify examples of each partner's "life culture." How are your separate homes decorated, what types of music or food do you each prefer, what is your favorite television show or how do you like to spend time socializing with friends? One simple but powerful example of "life culture" that you each bring to the relationship is how your family celebrates Thanksgiving.

Major holidays can be the source of great tension for many new couples if there is a significant difference in their family cultures and the expectations they bring to the relationship about how to celebrate these events. Perhaps one partner grew up in a large, extended family that never missed the chance to gather as a family. Holidays throughout the year were cherished opportunities to get together and talk, laugh, cry, eat and generally have fun. On the other hand, if the other partner was an only child raised by a depressed mother and alcoholic father, holidays may have been dreaded. Obviously, in this case, as a new couple it is easy to pick how you want to spend holidays in your new relationship.

The key is to realize that differing family cultures are part of the unique traditions each of you brings to the new partnership. However, it is essential that you spend time talking about the places where there are significant differences in your respective family cultures to avoid problems even before they arise. Identify traditions from each of your family cultures that you want to integrate into the new partnership or decide on new traditions that you want to establish.

Just be sure to address the issues of culture and traditions *before* your mother calls and says, "You will be coming to *our* house for Thanksgiving, won't you?" If you don't start your own family traditions around the holidays, you may find yourself going to multiple holiday dinners in an attempt to please everyone. Yet, no one ends up happy, you resent the process as you hurry around town pretending to be hungry at each stop, and there is little to give thanks for except that the day is over. This is especially difficult if you both come from big families who love to gather and celebrate holidays. Again, negotiations and compromise are the keys to navigating this touchy situation in an attempt to find a solution that is a win-win.

The result of this issue for my wife and me is that we host the families for Thanksgiving every other year to allow our extended family to develop alternative plans or accept invitations from other relatives.

One other consideration about combining cultures is that typically the family's income will increase, as will the expenses. On average, female-headed households earn $26,164 a year, while male-headed households earn $41,138 a year due to the wage gap. Meanwhile, married households earn $56,827 a year. On the surface this may sound like a good thing. However, in planning the merger, it is essential that you both have a clarifying conversation about funding the marital venture as detailed in Chapter 4.

The challenge is to learn what you want the new culture of your combined enterprise to be… to progress from what the culture is now and to what you want it to be. This may mean more frank discussions, lots of negotiating, better planning and strategies, redoing your vision or objectives, taking classes, and so on. Below are just a few questions that you may want to consider to help you better navigate the merger process, before you hit an unplanned obstacle.

1. What material possessions do you own that you are not willing to give up when we combine our household furnishings?

2. How would you respond to an adult sibling or relative who needed to borrow money?

3. What holidays are most important to you and how do you like to celebrate them?

4. How much, if any, contact will you likely have with your ex-spouse?

5. How should we deal with disciplining our children from a previous marriage?

6. How do you feel about having friends of the opposite sex?

The next chapter deals with writing detailed job descriptions that encompass your new merged or acquired status. Having solved the problems that come with mergers and acquisitions will enable you to tackle more tactical elements of the relationship in chapters to come.

Chapter Highlights:

- *Figuring out whether you are merging different identities and cultures into one cohesive yet different couple, or whether you are acquiring more than just a spouse... or both*

- *Recognizing the challenges of intimate relationships and blended families in today's times*

- *Gaining an understanding of what it takes to integrate a blended family and combine life cultures*

TACTICAL: *Relating to or involving actions carefully planned and executed to achieve a specific result!*

Chapter 7—Job Descriptions for Couples: Who Does What and How!— Best Practice #6

"We have the Bill of Rights. What we need is a Bill of Responsibilities."—Bill Maher, comedy talk show host

Chapter Objectives:

1. Understand the importance of having clear and attainable job descriptions for both you and your partner.

2. Learn how to divide (and conquer) tasks and write detailed job descriptions for both of you.

> **Dear John,**
>
> My wife and I are having trouble dividing household tasks. We both work in demanding careers that require long hours and some travel. We are vigilant about making sure we spend quality time with our two grade-school age daughters. In fact, every minute we are at home, we are helping with homework, reading to the girls, or playing games and puzzles with them.
>
> The only problem is that we live in literal chaos! Our house is a pigsty, and we are always out of food and necessities. But neither of us wants to cut back or quit our jobs. What is a modern-day working couple to do?
>
> **Signed,**
> **Living on a Prayer in Pennsylvania**

Dishes, tasks, and daily chores

Taking a business approach to your partnership helps you protect the love and romance in your relationship. By taking away the things that typically erode these wonderful feelings, such as stress and resentment over household tasks, family disagreements, or financial burdens, you can focus on the fun and contentment of life. As unromantic and analytical as this book's ideas may seem, they are meant to help you identify and overcome the barriers to a successful relationship to ensure that you will have more emotional space to enjoy each other and operate like a team or true partnership. If you follow the steps in *The Business of Love*, the hard part will already be resolved!

The Living on a Prayer in Pennsylvania couple needs a very detailed plan to make their relationship and family work like a well-oiled machine. Read on to gain information on what they (and you) can do to take the chaos and arguments about tasks out of relationships.

One of the most important things you can do in a business or relationship of any sort is to have clear and attainable job descriptions for everyone involved. A job description allows you to have good role clarity as well as a clear understanding of how you are expected to perform your job. Both partners must contribute to a relationship, and the things you do on a daily basis, as part of your job description, make up this contribution.

In the business world, every employee, from the mail clerk to the CEO, has a job description, either in writing or at least based on the historical behavior of whoever did that job before them. Some job descriptions may not be formalized, but there's at least a list of tasks and responsibilities that are provided or discussed. Otherwise, a company would not work very efficiently, if at all. Managers and supervisors use these lists of tasks to analyze your performance and to recognize and compensate you.

It is for these very reasons that I think it makes perfect sense for you and your partner to purposefully write job descriptions to define what each of you will do daily to maintain the relationship. Still not convinced? Do you think your partner already has a clear idea of what you expect of him? Don't be so sure.

Work/life balance studies show that the most common sources of conflict between couples are about money, children or household chores.

These three issues all too often become chronic battlegrounds and take all the kindness and caring out of an intimate relationship. A real preventive measure against these conflicts is to develop a complete listing of all the recurring tasks that must be accomplished to run your relationship on a daily basis—and then work together to develop clear and attainable job descriptions that detail the roles for both you and your partner in fulfilling these tasks.

How to communicate expectations

In the business world, the conflicts are often similar in origin to those in intimate relationships. While these conflicts between employer and employee may stem from many reasons, the main source is unfulfilled expectations. You may frequently hear examples of this in your daily work environment:

"I expected you to have known better; you *are* a long-time employee!"

"No one else had a problem understanding what they were supposed to do!"

"You were at the meeting where it was discussed, so I don't know why you didn't get the message!" If you fail to tell someone what your expectations are, then you cannot anticipate your expectations will be fulfilled to your standards, if at all.

Fixing this problem is not as easy as it seems. Just because we live in the information age with a myriad of communication choices doesn't mean that we've gotten any better at clearly talking or listening to each other; we all still assume far too much. In fact, communicating effectively has gotten even more difficult because we have too many opportunities to say the wrong thing, to be misinterpreted, or to forget to say what is important.

For example, as a consultant, I will often begin a meeting, workshop, or retreat by having the participants (in small groups) ask each other a key question like, "What do you expect most out of today's meeting, from this initiative, or during your training session?" One person from the group then reports the group's findings, so that the others may see if the communication was delivered correctly and whether their expectations are aligned with what is planned. This is an attempt to address the biggest source of frustration and conflict in business relationships today: unfulfilled expectations, as mentioned above.

As another way to make this point, I will often go to the projector and turn the lens to defocus the image on the screen (a metaphor for the way people see and interpret things differently if they are not clearly spelled out). If roles and responsibilities are left fuzzy, then they are open for multiple interpretations, and this often sets the stage for conflict. **So, be sure to get your relationship in focus!**

The upside of these exercises is that you start out with the commitment to communicate clearly with each other, knowing fully what is expected of one another. To have an effective partnership, it is important that you match competencies and motivations with the tasks that need to be accomplished and the roles that must be fulfilled. In an orchestra, the flute player knows she won't be playing the kettledrum. In the same way that a place kicker knows he won't be playing quarterback in the next game, a good partnership needs strong "role clarity" so that both partners will work toward a specific set of common objectives by matching the tasks with the competencies of each partner. At the same time, good partners pitch in when needed and never adopt the "it's not my job" attitude!

In the past, especially in the case of our parents and their parents, household tasks were usually based on gender-specific job descriptions that clearly defined men's work and women's work, regardless of competencies. In times past, when work involved hard manual labor, it made sense that men would do the "heavy lifting"—but women played an equally important role in performing manual tasks within their abilities. Now, thanks to modern conveniences, labor-saving appliances, and the fact that most of us live in suburbs, not on farms, the basis for performing tasks has changed.

In business, it would be rare for someone to be given a task based solely on gender. Of course, if that did happen, there would be grounds for a gender discrimination lawsuit. Yet, couples do the exact same "illegal" thing all the time at home. Studies continually underscore the fact that most working women believe the household work is to be shared with their spouses. Men may agree with that in theory, but in practice, women are still doing the bulk of those household tasks, especially the care and feeding of children. Men are simply not holding up their end of the bargain.

The core competencies of any marriage include skills in life management, communication, negotiations and problem solving, sound mental and physical health, child rearing, romance, and intimacy—yes, being romantic and intimate are skills that can be learned or enhanced.

In *The Business of Love*, relationships are driven by competency-based job descriptions. Each task is to be performed by the person who is the most competent, skilled, and motivated to perform them, regardless of gender. The man may cook and the woman may handle the finances. The man may garden and the woman may do the plumbing. The woman may do the travel planning and the man may be in charge of the social activities. The key is to break the stereotypical molds and match the task with the person most qualified to do the job: doing so makes sense in business, so why not at home?

In addition, if you have children, keep in mind that you are modeling key values and showing the children a certain philosophy of life by the tasks you choose and how you perform them. What kind of role model do you want to be for your children? What message do you send to your son when he sees you sitting on the couch watching TV while his mother is the only one ever cleaning the house (even though you both work full time)? Does this fit with your vision? Is this the happy life described in your vision statement for you, your partner and your children?

Here's another reality check: How do you think your partner will feel after years of doing all the tasks she loathes and you refuse to share? Do you think she'll feel kindly toward you for not lifting a finger to help with the most unpleasant or mundane chores? Relationships are based on cause and effect—and what you get is a direct result of what you give (or don't give).

Think back in your work experience to a time when you've seen a colleague or team member not pulling his weight or doing her fair share. How did that make you react? You probably felt resentful and angry. Now think about your partner's feelings when she does more than her fair share of work while you wonder why "she's lost that lovin' feeling!" I promise you that conflicts will arise if you and your partner do not mutually determine equitable job descriptions.

Elements of your work job description

It helps to look at your own job description from your place of work (if you have one). What are some of the common elements described in it? First, it may typically reference larger responsibilities, such as overseeing marketing, sales, operations, training, etc. Then, it probably focuses on specific tasks, such as implementing a process-improvement system, providing training programs, managing the budget or a profit-and-loss statement for the department, or overseeing the development of online content for the company's website. In other words, it states your larger responsibilities in the organization and then the specific tasks to make that larger role successful.

It works the same way with your relationship responsibilities. First, you decide who is doing the larger tasks like maintaining the household, taking care of the children, caring for the pets or the ailing parents, financial planning, etc. Then, you can move into more specific tasks, figuring out who does what around the house as well as outside of it.

Sample corporate job description for a Sales Account Manager

The account manager's individual responsibilities include, but are not limited to, the following:

1. *Plan and prioritize personal sales activities and customer/prospect contact towards achieving agreed business aims, including costs and sales—especially managing personal time and productivity.*

2. *Plan and manage personal business portfolio/territory/ business according to an agreed market development strategy.*

3. *Manage product/service mix, pricing and margins according to agreed aims.*

4. *Maintain and develop existing and new customers through appropriate propositions, ethical sales methods, and relevant internal liaison to optimize quality of service, business growth, and customer satisfaction.*

5. *Use customer and prospect contact activities tools and systems, and update relevant information held in these systems.*

6. *Plan/carry out/support local marketing activities to agreed budgets and timescales, and integrate personal sales efforts with other organized marketing activities, e.g., product launches, promotions, advertising, exhibitions and telemarketing.*

7. *Respond to and follow up on sales inquiries using appro- prate methods.*

8. *Monitor and report on market and competitor activities and provide relevant reports and information.*

9. *Record, analyze, report and administer according to systems and requirements.*

10. *Communicate, liaise, and negotiate internally and externally using appropriate methods to facilitate the development of profitable business and sustainable relationships.*

11. *Attend and present at external customer meetings and internal meetings with other company functions necessary to perform tasks and aid business development.*

12. *Attend training to develop relevant knowledge, techniques and skills.*

13. *Adhere to health and safety policy, and other requirements relating to care of equipment.*

14. *Other tasks as assigned!*

Writing your marital job description

To get started, think of your relationship as an organization that has you and your partner in the executive roles—maybe Chairman and President or CEO and COO or co-CEOs or co-Presidents or Partners. The title is not as important as the concept that you are equally sharing the tasks and the authority. Next, review the dimensions and objectives for your relationship, created in Chapter 3, to provide structure to the development of your job descriptions. All your previous hard work will now start to pay off. These dimensions and objectives will serve as a basis for the various tasks and responsibilities that need to be taken care of in your household and to manage your life together.

When you write your job descriptions, you can either do it separately or together. Choose the way that works best for you as a couple. You probably have a good idea as to how you work best after working on the vision and objectives or developing your brand.

Write your own overview of what role(s) you've agreed to take on and have your partner do the same. This will provide a strong start to tackling the more specific responsibilities in the next section.

We have now arrived at the concrete elements of this relationship model. In other words, we have moved beyond the conceptual and strategic issues that can be difficult to determine and combine, and are now into the concrete issues that affect couples on a daily basis. The Example Worksheet below is provided to help you and your partner develop an inventory of the tasks that need to be performed as part of your relationship job description. Please note that you will also use these tasks in the next chapters on performance feedback and compensation and benefits planning.

This Example Worksheet shows a sampling of the routine tasks necessary to sustain a typical relationship and family. Consider starting with a blank page and use this list to stimulate your thinking, as you brainstorm a comprehensive list that reflects your actual circumstances. Next, consider adding several columns, as shown, and place a check in the appropriate column to indicate whom you think should perform each task or how it should be handled. Then sit with your partner and compare your lists to see where you agree and where you will need to discuss, compromise or negotiate differences.

Also, in preparation for an activity in the chapter on

compensation and benefits, try to estimate the number of hours involved in performing each task you have listed on a monthly basis and the cost of paying someone to accomplish each of these tasks.

EXAMPLE – Partner Job Description Monthly Planning Worksheet										
Job Description Category / Task:	A	B	C	D	E	F	G	H	I	J
	His	Hers	Ours	Rotate	Negotiate	Outsource	Neither	Don't know	# of Hours	Est. $ Cost
CHILDREN										
changing diapers			√						2	$35
ensuring children perform their chores	√									
HOUSEHOLD CHORES										
maintaining computer, printers								√	3	$20
cleaning the bathroom					√				4	$50
ERRANDS										
dry cleaning	√								1	$125
filling prescriptions						√				$35
FOOD										
buying groceries					√				2	$500
cooking				√					12	$100

FINANCES										
paying bills	√								2	n/a
banking				√					1	n/a
PETS										
veterinary care for the pets						√			1	$10
washing the dog			√						1	n/a
FAMILY MANAGEMENT										
planning trips & vacations			√						1	n/a
maintaining family calendar								√	1	n/a

This Partner Job Description Planning worksheet is available in the Workbook that accompanies this book and can be found at www.thebusinessoflove.org

An added word on outsourcing

Many organizations have systematically outsourced to external vendors all but those tasks that they feel are "mission-critical." It is okay to consider doing the same in your relationship. Use modern technology to make your life easier. The Internet and an explosion of entrepreneurs have resulted in a never-ending list of services that you can buy if you and your partner cannot agree on or choose not to perform them. You may pick from doggie day care to in-home chefs, from online banking to on-demand laundry services, from part-time nannies to personal trainers, from professional complainers who act as your consumer advocate to

111

"honey do" handyman services. I even heard the other day of a service that will potty-train your child.

So, you and your partner need only to agree on what is mission-critical to the relationship. I assure you that the list is short, leaving what is *not* mission-critical to be seriously considered for outsourcing. Remind each other that these tasks are not cast in stone and will predictably change over time. You can always go back, revisit, and change them next month or next year.

Fun Exercise: To make sure you don't lose sight of your partner's valuable contribution and hard work, consider switching roles. As the saying goes, "Walk a mile in my shoes." Spend an hour, day or week in the other person's job. Sleep on the other side of the bed. Switch cars for a month. Change your routine! It is always good to understand what goes on in your partner's daily life. And it's a good way to achieve greater intimacy through greater understanding!

Chapter Highlights:

- *Recognizing the benefits of sharing household tasks with your partner, particularly if you both work outside the home*

- *Creating job descriptions and a detailed task list for both partners*

- *Preventing, reducing or eliminating conflicts over household chores*

- *Learning the importance of shared household responsibilities to maintain the intimacy and kindness of your long-term relationship*

TACTICAL: *Relating to or involving actions carefully planned and executed to achieve a specific result!*

Chapter 8—Relationship Feedback— Best Practice #7

"Don't lower your expectations to meet your performance. Raise your level of performance to meet your expectations. Expect the best of yourself, and then do what is necessary to make it a reality."—Ralph Marston, motivator and teacher.

Chapter Objectives:

1. Learn how to give and receive positive rein-forcement.

2. Practice how to redirect behavior in a produc-tive manner.

3. Set up a feedback process for you and your partner.

Dear John,

I've been married to my college sweetheart for seven years now. We really work well as a team, knowing what each one needs to do to keep our lives running smoothly. This is important because we are about to have our third child. I should mention it's a third boy, so you can imagine how tightly our ship has to be run.

The problem is that when one of us slips up or doesn't have time to do one of his or her chores, a HUGE fight ensues. My husband is prone to giving very harsh feedback that really makes me feel like I am a child. So in turn, I throw harsh criticisms back at him. It is totally unproductive, but we just don't know how to stop the vicious cycle. Do you have any advice for us?

Signed,
California Screamin'

Successful relationship feedback

It sounds like California Screamin' and her husband may have done a good job with writing job descriptions, but they now need some help giving each other productive feed-back. Once your job descriptions of roles and responsibili-ties in your relationship are clearly defined, it is time to dis-cuss the best way to provide feedback about how well each of you is fulfilling your job description, as shown in the Job Description Planning Worksheet in the previous chapter.

114

If you are doing the things that you and your partner agreed on in the last chapter, there should be few problems. We all make mistakes and slack off on our tasks now and then. And when we do, the feedback we often get is highly negative and sounds like this: "How many times do I have to ask you to pick your socks up off the floor?" or "You are no better a father than your own father was."

To avoid this kind of unproductive and damaging feedback, it is important to establish a productive process that does not have to be something you dread. This way when you have your marital meetings and retreats as described in Chapter 10, you'll have fewer negative things to discuss and a lot more positive accomplishments to celebrate.

For lack of a better word, "behavior" is used in the context of The Business of Love to describe how each of you is fulfilling your job description. Call it what you like, just be sure to not avoid talking about doing what you said you would do… it's about honesty and integrity in your job performance.

Now, let's look at how to provide positive feedback when your partner meets or exceeds expectations and how to successfully redirect behavior that falls short of expectations without diminishing your partner's self-concept. In most long-term relationships, spouses remember to compliment their partner every now and then. A husband will tell his wife she looks pretty, that he likes her hairstyle, or that she cooked a nice meal. A wife will tell her husband he did a good job mowing the lawn, or that he looks handsome today, or congratulate him on his promotion. These are very simple messages that all human beings need to feel appreciated or loved.

However, relationship feedback in the context of *The Business of Love* is more specific than a simple compliment. If you are going to take the time to provide feedback about how your partner has performed a task that is part of his or her job description, make sure that it really counts. Instead of simply saying, "Thanks for help in the kitchen," offer more descriptive and useful information. Try saying something like this: "The pantry looks great, it's so clean and organized… it's sure great to have your help with the work around the house!" The more descriptive and precise you are with the positive feedback, the more powerful the impact.

When giving feedback, be sure to use a common set of agreed upon standards, perhaps determined in writing your objectives or identified in your job description. For example, if you followed the steps in Chapter 3 on writing objectives, you might have discussed the dimension on Spirituality where you may have identified a core set of values and a code of conduct. This set of values and code of conduct can be the standard by which you evaluate each other's performance. The key is to have a unified set of standards that both partners use as the basis for feedback.

In a business setting, one key to effective feedback is when your supervisor's opinion is based on a common set of company values that serve as the basis for all behavior within the organization. Feedback is not given on a whim, based on the supervisor's mood, or impacted by bias or prejudice. It is consistent over time and is based on what behaviors are seen and heard, and whether or not these behaviors model company values.

At home, instead of just saying to your wife, "thanks for being a great mom," a good praising message would be, "I really appreciate how much patience you have with the kids on their math homework… because of you, I know our kids will get a good education."

In addition, it is important to note that a good praising message is typically a monologue, not a discussion. In telling your partner why you think a certain behavior is positive and productive, the most to expect is for your partner to give a simple "Thank you" or "You're welcome." You and your partner need to work on accepting each other's praising messages without debate and without discounting the significance of what is being acknowledged.

We all need to learn to do a better job of accepting praise and positive feedback. All too often, positive feedback is seen as a set up for something bad. It's natural to become suspicious, and wonder what the person really wants or to get ready for "the other shoe to drop!" Surprisingly for some, it is easier to accept criticism than to let the praise soak in and to truly accept the feedback as something we earned and deserve. If freely accepting positive feedback for yourself is difficult, it may mean that you don't give it freely either. Remember the best work you can do for the relationship is the work that you do on yourself… so get to work on overcoming barriers to being more open with your praise and recognition of your partner, if this is an issue.

Praising

When I conduct feedback training in businesses, I often ask a worthy and respected employee in the workshop to come up to the front of the room and then ask the other employees to give genuine comments on their actual experiences with their colleague, in the form of a very brief praising message. "Nicole, I really appreciate that every time I contact you about production schedules, you get right back to me. It shows that you are responsive and in support of our company value of teamwork. Thanks!" There is no further discussion—no ifs, ands or buts. It is just that simple.

Changing the context

The most important part of giving praising messages, especially if it is uncharacteristic of your typical behavior, is to provide a context for your new behavior so your partner will not be suspicious. Tell your partner that you are going to be acting differently from now on.

Let's say, for example, that you hear a message about the importance of keeping romance alive in a long-term relationship at your place of worship. Feeling a bit guilty, you take the message to heart and decide to stop on your way home from work and buy flowers for your spouse since you have not done this in quite awhile.

Without a proper context for your new behavior, when you proudly present the flowers to her, the first thing she might say is "OK, what did you do wrong?" Instead, if you had told her beforehand that you were impacted by the message and were going to actively work to rekindle the romance, she would have a different context for your new behavior and not have been suspicious—instead, she is more likely to be delighted with the flowers. She simply needed a new context for your unexpected behavior, a simple explanation about why you are going to be acting differently!

Another thing to consider is that praising messages do not have to be face-to-face. You can give praising messages in an email, text message, voice mail, or hide a card in her suitcase before she leaves on a business trip. Giving a praising message doesn't have to be time-consuming. Use technology as another means to keep the romance alive.

Redirecting

As you can imagine, trying to redirect your partner's behavior can be more challenging and complex. Be sure to give your feedback when your partner has done something that does not meet the expectations of their job description, or is outside your shared religious beliefs, or does not fit with the core values that you both may have established when setting relationship objectives in Chapter 3. Unlike praising, a redirecting message is meant to be a two-way discussion or dialogue. You will deliver your message, but then your partner needs to respond so you both can work on developing a mutually acceptable solution. However, before jumping to conclusions and prematurely setting the stage for a redirecting discussion, there are some questions you might consider *before* even talking with your partner:

1) Does your partner know the behavior does not meet your expectations?
2) Does your partner know what you want or value instead?
3) Are there obstacles beyond his or her control?
4) Does your partner know how to do what you want?
5) Could your partner do it if he or she wanted to?

If you consider all these questions and still end up with the realization that you need to talk with your partner about their behavior, here are some recommended steps to follow!

Delivering the redirecting message

1. Setting the stage—Ask your partner for a few minutes to talk about something that has been bothering you. If possible, deliver your message as soon as you can after the undesired behavior has occurred. Be sure not to ambush your partner; set up a meeting time that works for you both, just as you would do at work.

2. Sharing your observations—Remember to describe the specific behavior and how it does not seem to be in keeping with what you both value. Example: "Three times this week I heard you get angry with Billy because he couldn't understand his math homework."

3. Explaining your expectations—Be specific and tell your partner the specific behavior you want instead. "I'd like to see you be more patient

with him when he doesn't get the math homework figured out right away."

4. Listen to your partner's response—When it comes time for your partner to respond, it is likely that the response will be defensive, even if you try not to sound accusatory. The odds are high that your partner will feel guilty, frustrated or inept. It is natural to try to justify a behavior and explain it away. Listen patiently and let your partner have his or her say. After all, you might learn something that you did not know that explains the behavior. Ask clarifying questions, "Is there something that gets in the way of being patient with him?"

5. Develop a solution—With your partner's input, negotiate a realistic and mutually agreed upon solution to the behavior that you are trying to redirect. Be patient and work together to generate possible solutions. People are more likely to comply with solutions they help create. If they cannot or will not offer solutions, make your own suggestions about how the behavior might be redirected. "Should we trade off on helping with homework for a few weeks?" "Is there something I can do for you to make this go more smoothly?" Remember, the key is to focus not on who is right, but instead on what is right, and in this example, what is right for your son!

6. Follow-up—All redirecting discussions usually include follow-up to ensure that the behavior

has changed or is improving. Put a date on your calendar and plan to talk with your partner in a day, week or a month to review progress. If there has been improvement, reinforce the new behavior with positive feedback. But do not expect perfection! If the behavior does not change, schedule another session. Old habits die hard, and it may take several sessions before the undesirable behavior is successfully redirected.

Giving relationship feedback

Now that you understand how to give both praising and redirecting messages about a single behavior, we can move on to the all-important comprehensive feedback process. Typically, in the business environment, the formal performance feedback process is disliked and rarely done effectively. Most research shows that neither the person giving nor the person getting the feedback likes the process. All too often, performance feedback at work fails to provide meaningful information that can be turned into actions or is so vague that it offers little differentiation between poor and excellent performance.

Regardless of these commonly held beliefs, if done correctly, it can be very satisfying and rewarding to hear concrete examples and specific ratings of how well you are performing your job. If a company's employees are performing well, you can bet that business is likely to be successful, too. The opposite is also true: business failure is often due, in part, to employees who are not performing their jobs well.

Ideally, an employee's annual performance feedback is based on his or her job description. If an employee is fired for failing to perform a job he or she was never asked to do, it may result in a complaint or even a lawsuit. Similarly, it is not fair to criticize your partner for not performing a task or meeting a standard that person never agreed to fulfill.

Therefore, setting up clear expectations for how each of you will perform your jobs and responsibilities is a key element to a successful relationship. Talk about your job descriptions and make sure you each understand to what standard these tasks are to be completed.

For instance, if you've taken on cleaning the bathrooms once a week, discuss what your idea of a clean bathroom is. If your partner is a perfectionist or clean freak with a contamination phobia, make sure you can agree on a standard of cleanliness. Additionally, make sure you can live with how your partner will perform her tasks. The more specific you can be about expectations, the less likely it is that you'll fight over various interpretations of performance.

If you are responsible for grocery shopping, make sure you know what specific items your family members need to have for their daily lives or how to know when it is time to purchase groceries. Or if you are in charge of helping the kids with homework, make sure you and your partner are clear as to how much help and time you plan to offer. Once the standards are set, you can easily fold them into a regular relationship feedback process.

Creating a relationship feedback form

In your place of employment, your organization may use some type of standardized form that your supervisor asks you to fill out on yourself before your regular feedback meeting. This is a good idea for you and your partner as well. It gives you an idea as to the areas in which you think you fall behind or excel before you see your partner's opinions. When you compare forms, you may be surprised to learn that your partner thinks you are doing a good job in areas that you didn't feel were your best efforts. Or you may be perfectly aligned.

The easiest way to begin the feedback process is to use the job descriptions that you (hopefully) developed from Chapter 7 as a basis for the feedback you give your partner, as shown below. In Part 1 of the example form, consider each task on the list that is part of your or your partner's job description. Then think back over an agreed upon period of time, preferably 90 to 180 days, and then select the number that most accurately reflects how well you feel that you or your partner has completed this task. In Part 2, be sure to add comments to further clarify any task where you might have given a "Does not meet expectations" or "Exceeds expectations!" For example, take the grocery shopping duty. A score of **3** would mean you are never in want for anything when you go into the kitchen, and a score of **1** could mean you are always out of bananas and toilet paper.

In our household, we are often out of milk and end up running out to the store to get it just for our coffee in the morning. Since Charlotte has agreed to buy groceries as part of her job description, she gets lower marks for this responsibility! While we joke about this and approach these types of discussions in a caring, lighthearted and positive manner, we both still know that avoiding dealing with disappointments in the little things can lead to bigger issues going unresolved as well.

Remember that the focus of this activity is to provide feedback to your partner. Just as in business, it is meant to be a tool to strengthen the relationship, clarify expectations, and ensure that the day-to-day tasks of being in a relationship do not get in the way of an ever-deepening friendship built on trust, mutual respect, intimacy and forgiveness.

It may be uncomfortable the first time you give and receive the feedback, but look at it as taking the more proactive route by having a systematic way to give feedback on agreed-to tasks. You will bypass the unproductive comments and criticisms that come from weeks (or maybe years) of frustration and anger stemming from unfulfilled expectations or poor performance. Approaching the feedback process with a caring attitude and a spirit of friendly cooperation will go a long way toward establishing regular feedback as one of the most powerful and positive events that you and your partner can build into the foundation of your relationship.

THE BUSINESS OF LOVE

Relationship Feedback – Part 1

Performance Checklist	Does not meet expectations	Meets expectations	Exceeds expectations
1. buying groceries	√		
2. paying bills			√
3. caring for the pets		√	
4. feeding the children			√
5. maintaining computer, printers		√	
6. changing diapers			√
7. reading bedtime stories			√
8. cleaning the bathroom	√		
9. dry cleaning			√
10. vacuuming			√
11. cooking		√	
12. yard work			
13. car maintenance	√		
14. house maintenance	√		
15. banking			√
16. investing		√	
17. maintaining family calendar			√

126

18. driving children to school			
19. driving children to after-school events			√
20. taking care of prescriptions			√
21. changing the bedding			√
22. laundry			√
23. sending cards and gifts			√
24. cleaning the garage		√	
25. setting up date night		√	
26. scheduling time with children and grandchildren			√
27. clean outside porches	√		
28. washing the dog		√	
29. bathing the children			√
30. taking the garbage out		√	
31. maintaining the pool		√	

Relationship Feedback—Part 2
Additional comments

Exceeding expectations:
You are the best parent I have ever seen. You are more patient, accepting and loving than I could ever be

Meets expectations:
Thanks for finding the time to cook in the middle of everything else you are juggling

Does not meet expectations:
We are often out of milk and dog food which makes it difficult on me when trying to make breakfast for the kids and I feel guilty when I only have table scraps to feed the dog

This Relationship Feedback form is available in the Workbook that accompanies this book and can be found at www.thebusinessoflove.org

Formalize the process

Establish a mutually convenient time, duration, and frequency for your feedback sessions—at least one or two hours every 90 to 180 days. Be sure to plan ahead and mark a date on your calendar so you don't forget to prepare yourself, get a babysitter, and so forth. The frequency of these meetings will be based on how important feedback is to your relationship. If you are married with children and you both work hectic schedules, it might be more important for you to meet more frequently, even if for only a few minutes at a time. Meeting once a year may be enough if you are in a long-term relationship and are empty-nesters living a stable and leisurely lifestyle. If you are somewhere in between, you may want to meet twice per year. It's up to you. Choose the frequency that is best for you and your partner's needs. Complete the forms on each other in advance, and then sit down and go through each item together. See Chapter 10, Meetings and Retreats, for more information on conducting these types of meetings. Remember that the formal feedback process is supplemented with praising and redirecting discussions that occur on a regular basis, as necessary or appropriate. While this ongoing feedback is not a replacement for the formalized process, it is also best not to wait long periods to provide feedback.

If done correctly, there will be no surprises when you have your formal face-to-face meeting. Because you have agreed to do certain tasks to a specific standard, it is unlikely that you will be shocked to get a low score on something you haven't been accomplishing well. Similarly, you will likely be delighted to hear positive feedback and receive high scores in the areas of your job description where you feel most competent.

Finally, keep in mind that it is important to remain flexible with the various tasks on each job description. Circumstances change, motivation will vary, competencies may increase or someone may tire of doing a particularly mundane, difficult or unpleasant task. Remember that negotiation and compromise are critical to the long-term success of the relationship. Don't let conflict and tension about daily roles and responsibilities sap the romance and commitment from your partnership.

Chapter Highlights:

- *Learning how to give positive, praising reinforcement*
- *Learning how to redirect behavior in a productive manner*
- *Setting up a process for you and your partner to give regular feedback*

TACTICAL: *Relating to or involving actions carefully planned and executed to achieve a specific result!*

Chapter 9—Compensation and Benefits— Best Practice #8

"You know you are on the road to success if you would do your job, and not be paid for it."—Oprah Winfrey, entertainer and entrepreneur

Chapter Objectives:

1. Discover what motivates us to be in the relationship so that we can ensure our motivation will continue.

2. Measure the monetary value you bring to your relationship and quality of life.

3. Create a "benefits package" for your relationship.

4. Sign a contract that spells out all the important things you want and need from your relationship.

Dear John,

I am a newlywed with just one year of marriage under my belt. So many things have changed for the worse in this year that I am not sure I chose the right person to spend my life with. Our sex life has taken a complete nose-dive, and I feel little support from my wife when discussing my job and career aspirations.

We are discussing whether we want to start a family, but I can't see bringing kids into a relationship that has no upside for me. How can I talk to her about getting what I need (and what I think she wants) so badly from our marriage?

Signed,
The Neglected Husband
Kansas City, MO

Getting paid

It is likely, Neglected Husband, that if you are not getting what you want out of your relationship, neither is your partner. But we all have different needs from a relationship, so you might start by taking stock of how you get compensated in the relationship and then clearly communicating that to your partner.

I know what you are likely asking yourself right now, "Compensation? I get money for being in a relationship?" Well, you may not get cash-based compensation, but if you have a healthy and intimate relationship, you do get something that money cannot buy—an "emotional paycheck." This chapter will explore the compensation and benefits of being in a successful, long-term relationship.

Motivators

The first thing we need to do is realize the motivation behind the things we choose to do as well as the relationships we choose to be in. While the motive may not be evident at the time, we always have reasons for our actions— behavior is the physical manifestation of an underlying motive. If you grew up in a positive, loving home where dad was the breadwinner, mom was the homemaker, and it seemed to work well for them, the odds are that you will be motivated to recreate that model in your own relationship despite your own claims to the contrary.

If, on the other hand, your parents were both troubled, dysfunctional alcoholics, you will understandably be motivated to build a relationship as different as possible from that of your own parents. Understanding the motives for your relationship can be illuminating and unsettling at the same time. For the purpose of this chapter, let's agree that there is a payoff for your relationship even if you don't know what it is now. But you will need to understand what the motivations are to ensure that you keep getting "paid!"

In business, how to motivate yourself and others is often the subject of debate. While there is no simple or clear formula for what will increase motivation in others, it is accurate to say that different employees are motivated by different things.

First, many employers think they know what motivates their employees and will often cite more money, greater job security or opportunities for promotion. All of these things cost the company money. Interestingly enough, studies show that employees often cite a very different list of motivations for working, such as being appreciated for the quantity or quality of work performed, a feeling of "being in on things," help with personal problems, or the loyalty of their supervisor. All of these elements have an emotional base and do not cost money.

I give this information to my clients because what truly motivates an employee to give his or her all at work is not always perceived correctly by the employer. The same thing applies to our partners. While you may think you know what motivates her, the truth is that, unless you explore your motivation for marriage and discuss it with your partner, it is unlikely that you know what she (or you, for that matter) needs in her "emotional paycheck" to feel rewarded.

So take a few minutes to think about what motivates you to be with your partner, what motivates you to stay in the relationship, and what you think will keep you motivated in the future? Ask your partner to do the same and then tell each other what you have (re)discovered. Be forewarned: you may be surprised or even shocked to hear what's really going on in your partner's mind.

Determining your "emotional paycheck"

In business, you get paid for the work that you perform based on the value you contribute to your company's bottom line. In *The Business of Love*, it is similar since you add value to the relationship based on the tasks you perform in your job description. Just for fun, you may want to figure out the value of what you do for the relationship that you don't actually get paid to do. Consider adding up the costs of outsourcing the tasks on your job description from Chapter 7. Go back to your Job Description Planning and be sure to complete column "I," where you estimate the number of hours you spend performing that task on a monthly basis. Then complete column "J," where you estimate what it would cost to pay someone to perform that task if you had to buy the service on the open market.

Estimating the number of hours will likely be easier than estimating the cost to buy that service, but accuracy is not the point. Instead, the point is to see your relationship in a different light and to understand that you contribute to *and* derive value from your relationship. In *The Business of Love*, each spouse is valued for the contribution he or she makes to the relationship, whether bringing home a six-figure income or staying at home to raise children.

In reality, these contributions may not have the same monetary value, but it is critical that they be seen as having equal emotional value. This is the worth of your contribution to and compensation for the relationship, something you can feel empowered by and proud of. In *The Business of*

Love, there is no need to argue about who contributes more... partners are different, but both contribute equally and are compensated equally.

Just for fun, see the sample chart below as a guide to come up with the total amount of your relationship compensation. NOTE: You may simply have to guesstimate for some of the categories, though the ranges provided are based on national figures for some of the more well-known service categories. You may be surprised or even shocked once you determine the bottom line of your contribution—just be glad you do not have to pay taxes on this compensation!

This Relationship Compensation Calculation Worksheet is available in the Workbook that accompanies this book and can be found at www.thebusinessoflove.org

Relationship Compensation – Calculation Worksheet		
Task	*Monthly cost*	*Annualized Cost*
1) House cleaning— maid service	$100 - $200	$1,200 - $2,400
2) Chauffeur— family and children	$400 - $600	$4,800 - $7,200
3) Automobile care & maintenance	$50 - $200	$600 - $2,400
4) Personal assistant—*includes maintaining schedule, running errands, buying gifts, social event planning, etc.*	$1,000 - $2,000	$12,000 - $24,000

5) Nanny—daycare	$1,600 - $2,000	$19,200 - $24,000
6) Yard work—gardening	$90 - $120	$1,080 - $1,440
7) Bookkeeper—*maintaining personal finances—includes banking, maintaining financial software, filing taxes*	$100 - $300	$1,200 - $3,600
8) Pet care	$240 - $300	$2,880 - $3,600
9) Laundry—*wash, dry, and fold service—excluding dry cleaning*	$50 - $60	$600 - $720
10) Inventorying, buying, and stocking groceries	$50 - $100	$600 - $1,200
11) Food preparation	$500 - $1,000	$6,000 - $12,000
12) Pool & recreational equipment maintenance	$70 - $90	$840 - $1,080
13) Handyman—repair services	$300 - $400	$3,600 - $4,800
14) "Escort" Service—*8-10 days/nights monthly*	$2,500 - $5,000	$30,000 - $60,000
Sample marital compensation totals:	$7,000 - 14,070	$84,600 -$148,440

Developing your "benefits package"

On the other side of relationship compensation are the benefits you get from being in the relationship. In business, the benefits package encompasses the all-important items that customarily come with the job, such as health and dental insurance, pensions, retirement funds and 401Ks, holiday parties, travel and entertainment expense accounts, flexible hours, telecommuting, maternity leave, paid time off, and so on. In addition to these ready-made benefits, you also (hopefully) receive the benefit of increased self-worth, camaraderie with colleagues you respect, increased job knowledge, learning new skills, and feeling useful and valued.

The same feelings apply to a healthy and intimate relationship. Your benefits might be as simple as being loved and understood or having a satisfying sex life or daily companionship. Other benefits of being together can be such varied things as having a gourmet dinner companion or being with someone who shares your interest in taking adventurous trips. Perhaps you benefit by competing in who can be most romantic, or in sharing your faith journey, or in achieving financial serenity, and more.

Along with your emotional paycheck discussed earlier, you might consider coming up with a statement that describes your relationship "benefits package." For example, your statement could simply be, "As a result of marrying you, I will have a good father for my kids, a wonderful life of travel and adventure, no worries about money, and fun-filled days and nights." Another example could be, "The reason I am accepting this 'job' offer to be your partner in marriage is to feel love and support everyday as we live together, with romance, fulfilling sexual relations, and companionship as a part of our daily existence." It takes the vision of your relationship to a more individual, "what's in it for me" kind of level, which of course is why you are there in the first place—it is your motivation for being in the relationship.

Because the preferred benefits package can be unique for each individual in the partnership, it is hard to develop a general list of benefits that fits everyone. However, as you would when you negotiate with a potential new employer after they have extended you a job offer, here are some questions to consider to help identify what benefits are important to you and to serve as the basis for developing your relationship benefits package:

1. How do you want to be appreciated for the contribution of the "emotional paycheck" (calculated above) to the relationship?

2. What is the best method for your partner to show you that he/she loves you?

3. How do you prefer to celebrate special events, e.g., birthdays?

4. How do you like to be shown physical affection (in public)?

5. When you have done something that benefits your relationship in an extraordinary way, how would you like it to be acknowledged?

6. When you have had a particularly pressured and stressful day, how would you like your partner to show her or his empathy and support?

Once you have answered these and any other questions that you feel are pertinent to determining what you want in your benefits package, you can write a statement describing the benefits of your relationship, as it exists today. It is okay if this evolves over time.

The marital contract

"Those who can't be bothered to negotiate its details demean the grand institution of matrimony." - Nobel Laureate George J. Stigler (1982, Economics)

I heartily agree! Essentially, a marriage is an unwritten contract between you and your partner. The only unfortunate part is that all too often, because it is unwritten, it is vague, open to interpretation, selectively forgotten or rationalized away. Agreeing on a marital contract can be useful in making sure you both remember why it is you got into this relationship in the first place.

Many companies have employment contracts with their employees, particularly for senior management, that state the terms of the relationship and the rights each entity carries into the relationship. The major issues within an employee contract are compensation, tasks and responsibilities, performance evaluation, and a few other necessary legalities. We've already talked about many of these issues in *The Business of Love*, but now you may want to commit to them formally, in contract form. Please keep in mind that this is *not* a prenuptial agreement that spells out what happens to marital assets if the relationship fails. In *The Business of Love*, the marital contract is the foundation to ensure that your relationship is successful, productive and sustainable.

A contract can have strong similarities to the vows you said at your wedding or other meaningful things that have been said to each other along the way, especially in the commitment phase of your partnership. It could contain elements of your vision for the relationship and how you will maintain and nurture it. It could include a list of needs and wants (like your emotional paycheck and compensation package that you just detailed) and how you will satisfy each other's expectations for the relationship.

As an example, what follows is an edited excerpt from a sample marriage contract written by students at a community college and is now in the public domain. While it may have elements that are not relevant to your relationship, such as blended families and stepchildren, you may still find it a useful tool as a basis for developing your own relationship contract, or at least it may provide the basis for more intimate conservations with your partner.

This abbreviated Relationship Contract along with the extended version is available in the Workbook that accompanies this book that can be found at www.thebusinessoflove.org

RELATIONSHIP CONTRACT

My name:

My partner's name:

1. General statement about why we are getting married to each other with our general values and philosophy of marriage:

   - We need and want a healthy relationship and believe that we will be able to resolve difficulties as long as we have the motivation to do so. Motivation is essential for sustaining a marriage.

   - In our country, society has been structured around the family unit. Functional families are therefore the foundation of our communities. Successful marriages enable functional families.

   - Child-bearing is only the beginning of family life. After the time of child-bearing has passed, couples still must nurture their children and each other. Remarriage forms blended families which must nurture step-children, whether they are very young or adolescents. Even adult children like the nurturing continued.

   - We love and value each other. We each have knowledge of failed marriages. A sound, lasting marriage is still very appealing to each of us in spite of this. We feel that we and our children would benefit from the nurturing that we need and that this marriage would provide.

2. A description of specific behavior we plan and expect from each other in each of the following areas:

Money

- Each of us is entering the partnership free from debt. We plan to have a joint bank account.

- We will save the first 10% of our gross earnings plus interest in 401Ks at our place of employment for retirement. We plan to save an additional 5% for a mutually agreed-upon annual vacation planned together in advance, and to save another 5% of gross earnings for emergencies, and, if not needed, for a mutually planned expenditure.

- Taxes, property payments, utilities, food, property maintenance, transportation, insurance payments and church contributions will come from the joint bank account.

- Any loans or donations to friends or relatives will be mutually agreed upon in advance before being offered to the person in need.

Sex

- We agree that monogamous intimate relations between married people are essential for trust.

We will try to understand and respect the sexual desires of each other.

- We agree upon frequent sex for mutual enjoyment and fulfillment, and agree not to use it as a power-play in the marriage.

Careers

- We agree that, beyond financial necessity, careers provide healthy ego and social satisfaction.
- Present careers are to be maintained and any future career changes are to be mutually decided and supported.

Children

- We agree that resident and non-resident children need to be accommodated. We have agreed to accept each other's children.
- Duties and responsibilities for each blended family member are to be mutually planned and communicated to the children.
- We have also agreed to allow children, regardless of age, to spend time alone with the natural parent when needed. We will try to understand the extra nurturing given by the natural parent.

In-laws

- We have agreed to accept and respect our in-laws.

- We will alternate with families each year in order to keep up family traditions of participation in holiday dinners.
- Birthday parties, weddings, funerals and other special occasions will be attended when possible as a couple.

Residences

- We plan to agree to a principal residence in the community of the husband's career.
- If one of us should decide upon a career change, we will collaborate on a choice of residence.

Friends

- We agree to accept each other's friends, and have already accepted our friends of the past. Time and activities will be mutually planned and agreed upon.
- We'll each respect best friends of the other and allow for time alone with them when needed.

Recreation

- We have agreed to mutually plan and share vacations and other times of recreation.
- If one partner should wish to plan recreation with children alone, it will also be mutually agreed upon.

Religion

- One of us is Protestant and the other Catholic. We believe in the basic tenets of our respective religions, but are tolerant of, and will respect, the beliefs of our partner.

- We have agreed to the participation to some degree in our partner's religious tradition, and each expects reciprocation.

General Problem-Solving Techniques

- We have agreed to open discussion for at least ten minutes as problems surface to initiate steps for resolution. Then, individual contemplation for at least one hour before returning to open discussion.

- If this cannot be sustained, the discussion will be postponed for twenty-four hours, and then restarted. If this fails, outside counseling should be initiated.

Signed:

Partner 1_____Date: _____

Partner 2_____Date: _____

Do you feel the love?

By now, you have a good sense of what you and your partner need most out of your relationship to feel valued and "well-paid." You may even have a formal contract to prove it! You may also want to compare your results with your vision and objectives to ensure they are all aligned. At the end of it all, make sure these different elements of your emotional pay make you feel well compensated and abundantly rewarded. Remember, this chapter is simply about identifying your motives for being in the relationship. We all have them, and the more you know about yours, the better partner you can be.

In the next chapter, we will discuss meetings and retreats as an effective means to manage the day-to-day tasks of being in the relationship or as a special, dedicated period during which you will be reviewing your vision and objectives to evaluate how well your entire relationship enterprise is working. Now it's time to schedule a meeting or set the date for that all-important retreat to revisit all your hard work on *The Business of Love.*

Chapter Highlights:

- *Understanding what motivates you and your partner to be in the relationship*

- *Detailing your monetary contribution to the relationship and knowing the amount of your emotional paycheck*

- *Writing down the emotional benefits of being with each other*

- *Exploring options for writing a relationship contract as the basis for a long-term commitment*

TACTICAL: *Relating to or involving actions carefully planned and executed to achieve a specific result!*

Chapter 10—Meetings and Retreats— Best Practice #9

"Life is what happens while you're busy making other plans."—John Lennon, singer, musician, artist and writer

Chapter Objectives:

1. Introduce how to hold regular meetings to conduct the business of your relationship.

2. Understand the guidelines to running effective relationship meetings on a regular basis.

3. Plan an annual retreat to fully reevaluate and refuel your relationship.

Dear John,

I have a classic problem in my relationship. I've lived with a kind and generous man for 6 years now, but his lack of communication skills is a major problem. I get insecure about how our relationship is going on a daily basis. I've asked him to sit down and talk about it with me, but he can never find the time. When I do pin him down, our talks are all one way—I do all the talking.

There is so much going on with our relationship but I can't get him to give me any feedback about how he feels about me or our life together. I'm really having a hard time feeling good about the future. Is there anything I can do to get him to make time for me on a regular basis?

Signed,
Waiting for the Man
Colorado Springs, CO

Once again, I must encourage you to take the more difficult areas of your life and formalize them in a way that makes it almost routine to communicate with each other. Regular meetings and annual retreats will help to increase communications and help to ensure the long-term viability and sustainability of your relationship.

Let's do lunch

The common complaint from many employees in all

types of organizations is, "Meetings, meetings and more meetings! Sometimes it seems that rather than getting any real work done, all we do is attend meetings!" Interestingly enough, couples often complain of the opposite: that the partners are both so busy that they never find time to meet and really talk about what is going on in their lives and their relationship.

While we might all agree that there is always a need to improve communication through meetings, companies often actually damage communication by holding an endless series of unproductive meetings. It is no wonder that the idea of holding regular meetings with your partner might not sound like the most exciting way to spend time together.

However, in the best of circumstances, properly run meetings can be a highly effective method to keep the flow of communication strong, to move projects and ideas forward, and to conduct business. When a business meeting is managed the right way, it can create a better, more effective working environment.

The same can be said about relationship meetings. Holding regular meetings to conduct *The Business of Love* of your relationship is one of the most effective strategies to enhance satisfaction and prevent more serious problems in the future. While this proposition may make sense, our busy lives don't always allow for uninterrupted discussions about the everyday issues that must be managed between partners. Life does happen anyway, so you have a choice either to be purposeful in your interactions and communication patterns with your partner or to risk negative consequences.

Spontaneous and purposeful meetings

The fact is that you are most likely already having spontaneous meetings, like the typical passing discussions about your work schedule or activities at home during breakfast, on your cell phone on the way home from work, in a series of text messages, or in a string of emails. If you are having these discussions already, and if they are effective, don't abandon this approach. These informal, spontaneous discussions about your mom's health or your son's report card often get the job done. The bottom line is that you are taking the time amid all the distractions of life to talk about what is going on in your life.

While I encourage these spontaneous meetings whenever there's a need, I also would like you to consider the importance of setting up a purposeful, structured, face-to-face relationship meeting on a regular basis. For many couples, having a consistent meeting on the first and third Tuesday of the month (or whatever day suits you) brings a sense of comfort because each partner knows that there is a dedicated time set aside to talk about the minor and major issues of the relationship. These planned meetings are a time to talk about the business of the relationship, roles and responsibilities, upcoming events and general problems (excluding redirecting of behavior sessions about your partner's job performance).

In addition, the purposeful couple's meetings described here are different than the family discussions that you may already have at the dinner table and that possibly include the children. In these circumstances, you will normally stay in your parental role while avoiding those areas that are inappropriate to discuss in front of children, i.e., the business of the relationship. However, couples still need to dedicate meeting time to discuss the business of their relationship. It is similar to management holding an all-staff meeting followed by a separate executive meeting.

Guidelines for a purposeful couple's meeting

Certain techniques for running an effective meeting can be applied to your formal couple meetings, as follows:

1. Be sure to write an agenda.

2. Estimate the amount of time you will need to talk about any given topic on the agenda.

3. Describe the outcome you need when covering each agenda item.

4. Be sure to write down the decisions made and actions to be taken.

5. Keep the discussion focused on agenda items only—do not pad the meeting with other items unless there is mutual agreement.

6. Don't ambush—discussing problematic behavior is best set aside for a single-item meeting.

7. Be sure to start and end the meeting on time.

One last guideline: no multi-tasking allowed. Multi-tasking typically means doing several things at the same time, poorly. Consider how you would feel if, in the middle of lovemaking, your wife pulled out the checkbook and starting reconciling the bank statement? It just isn't a good idea. The same thing goes for when you and your partner are attending the couple's meeting. You need *uninterrupted* time to discuss the business of your relationship. The meeting is sacred, the time protected, the TV and phones off, and the children elsewhere.

In addition, if it is not already part of your job description, consider rotating the "facilitator" role so each of you takes responsibility for making these meetings valuable. See below for a sample agenda.

Sample Agenda: Monthly Couples Information Meeting
Jenny's Topics:
1. Kids' activities—5-7 minutes—need to agree which sports to support and how to integrate them into the family's overall schedule.
2. Bill payment—2 minutes—make the final decision to switch over to online bill payment.
3. Vacation plans—10 minutes—present the latest information about the beach vs. mountain trip, costs, accommodations, dates, etc.
4. Business trip—5 minutes—discuss conflicts with business travel and daughter's upcoming recital.
5. Gift-buying—2 minutes—decide what to buy for my brother's birthday.
Steve's Topics:
1. Weekend chores—3 minutes—determine the priority of the "honey do" list.
2. Investment planning—2 minutes—set the meeting with the estate planning attorney.
3. Car maintenance—5 minutes—decide what to do while the SUV is in the shop.
4. Upcoming house projects—10 minutes—present the estimated budget for the added deck and patio area; report the latest on getting the permit from the city.
5. Business trip—5 minutes—discuss conflicts with business travel and weekend softball game.

To keep meetings useful, be sure to occasionally take a few minutes at the end to evaluate the effectiveness of the meetings. Are they too far apart, not long enough, the wrong time of day, irrelevant, meaningful, productive? Don't be afraid to make adjustments to ensure the meetings remain of value to you both.

You can add intimate touches to these meetings, too. Start or end each meeting with a prayer or one positive life experience each of you has had since the last meeting. While having a redirecting discussion about a partner's job performance is off-limits, I encourage you to spontaneously give a praising message: "You know, we get so much done at these meetings because you are so good at keeping us focused on the important issues. Thanks for running these meetings." Or, "Thanks for doing all that research on vacations. It really helps us to narrow the choices to a few places. This will make our decision so much easier." See, it's easy— and it gives your partner something to feel good about. The key is to make the meetings something you look forward to each time.

Adding structure, reducing complexity

When you are discussing many different types of issues in a single meeting, it can add complexity that becomes disruptive. For instance, if you are discussing your daughter's poor grades and doing vacation planning in the same meeting, it can be hard to tackle such emotionally diverse issues in the same discussion.

Instead, consider planning the agenda in a sequence that

starts with the fun, simple, and easy issues before tackling those more challenging aspects of your relationship and family. Or do just the opposite, and save the fun stuff for last, to end on a positive note. Consider taking a break between the easy and challenging topics, or even plan on having two different meetings. In addition, consider the different types of meetings, and be sure to select the meeting format most appropriate for the items on the agenda. Do you need to make decisions, solve problems, share information, or do planning?

For instance, an informational meeting (again, see the sample agenda) could simply provide basic information as to what is going on in your life. A decision-making meeting could be to finalize a car purchase or to start planning a living trust. A problem-solving meeting may seek to address your son's problems at school. Planning meetings can be a fun time to plan vacations or brainstorm home improvement ideas.

You can also combine some of the meetings: for example, a mixture of information and making plans, or a mixture of finalizing the decision of which dental specialist to use and coming up with other solutions to your daughter's speech problems. Any combination can work, assuming one agenda item isn't so contentious that it overrides the other items on the agenda.

Retreat and recharge!

If meetings are about the day-to-day business of your relationship and family (like the objectives in each dimension of your relationship or the tasks on your job description), a retreat is a once- or twice-a-year getaway to fully reevaluate and refuel your relationship. It is truly a retreat from your daily life and is meant to be both positive and productive.

When businesspeople go away on a retreat, they get out of the office or they close the office for the day so there are no distractions. Companies often use this time to look at their long-range vision and to evaluate progress in meeting objectives, and to establish new targets for the business. At some retreats, companies ask their employees to come up with creative new ideas that could take the company in a different direction. Whatever the content of a business retreat, it usually focuses on the higher-level company issues rather than the daily business that a staff meeting would cover.

Marital retreats do not happen at the kitchen table or over email. They do not happen in the car on the way home from work together. A retreat is that special time to go away and just be with one another. Maybe you can find a special in the newspaper for a local hotel and spa, or maybe you'd prefer to camp out in the wilderness. If you have an annual vacation, there might be times during that break to also have your retreat (send your kids to the children's camp for the day). All you need is a copy of your vision statement and brand logo, objectives, job descriptions, performance feedback and each other.

You need to have a few dedicated large blocks of time to cover a prepared agenda: revisiting and reevaluating the vision and objectives, getting an update on the family's financial picture, and other long-term issues appropriate to your life (like caring for parents, having children, retiring, etc.). No matter where you go, make sure you have these blocks of time where no one will bother you, except perhaps for a waiter delivering room service.

At some time during this retreat, remember to schedule a formal performance feedback meeting, as mentioned in Chapter 8, and a discussion about your compensation and benefits, as mentioned in Chapter 9. Remember, during the mutual performance feedback discussion, there should be no surprises because, ideally, you both have been praising and redirecting throughout the year. The performance discussion is simply a summary of all the feedback you've given and received during those discussions over the past few months. In addition, this is the time to verify with your partner that you are still investing in the relationship by fulfilling the roles on your job description and that you are feeling sufficiently gratified by what you are receiving in return.

If you must stay at home to have your retreat, keep two important factors in mind:

1. You must send the kids away for the day.
2. Turn off the televisions, phones and all the other distractions of your normal daily life.

Try to create a different atmosphere in your home that does *not* include doing dishes or returning e-mail. Just as with the purposeful relationship meetings, be sure to evaluate the retreat to ensure it was helpful and a worthwhile investment in your relationship. Balance the "fun" and "work" sides of this valuable time away. If you need to modify things for next year's retreat, do so. Practice makes perfect!

I also encourage you to play and have fun between the big blocks of dedicated retreat time, especially if you engage in team-building efforts like snorkeling, couples massage, golfing, lovemaking, and so on. Think about what elements of your own company retreats you really liked and incorporate them, as appropriate.

Most of all, be sure to enjoy your time alone together and be romantic. Watch the sunset, take long walks, sit together in silence gazing at the ocean, and talk. I mean, really talk. The goal of your relationship (and this book) is for you to reach a level of intimacy with your partner that brings together the best of friendship and an ever-deepening love.

Chapter Highlights:

- *Recognizing the value of incorporating regular meetings into your life, no matter how busy you are*

- *Learning to run an effective formal meeting with your partner*

- *Planning your next retreat with your partner to recharge your relationship*

Chapter 11—
The Commencement

"Be who you are and say what you feel, because those who mind don't matter and those who matter don't mind."
—Dr. Seuss, author

> **Dear John,**
>
> I am thirty-two years old and about to get married to an amazing woman I've known for about a year. I do not want to be another divorce statistic like my parents. However, there is so much to learn and apply to making a relationship successful, where do I start?
>
> **Signed,**
> **Dazed and Confused**
> **Orlando, FL.**

Well, Dazed and Confused, the short answer to your question is, start with yourself. Use the strategies and exercises in this book to make yourself into the "right person" for the relationship. In fact, if you remember nothing else from *The Business of Love*, remember that the most important work you can do for your relationship is the work you do on yourself. It certainly helps to do the work simultaneously with your partner, fiancée or spouse, if you can, but it is not required.

The beginning of the rest of your relationship

You've made it through this book, but hopefully *not* untouched. Reading this book was not supposed to be just simply fun or easy… nothing worthwhile ever is. Feel proud of yourself for being open-minded enough to explore a different way to think about yourself and your relationship. *The number one obstacle to self-development is self-deception.* I think it would be hard to make it from cover-to-cover of this book and still be deceiving yourself.

By reading this book to the end, you have chosen to consider a new approach to relationships and perhaps *not* to

162

be another divorce statistic. You might also have recognized that you don't want to follow your parents' or grandparents' traditional model of relationships. Nor do you want to live a fantasy and pretend you are Romeo and Juliet (who both died in the play) living happily ever after. That's enough on what you *don't* want to do; let's discuss what you *do* want to do from here.

The Business of Love model for an intimate relationship provides a clear, straightforward approach to building or enhancing a long-term committed relationship. Coming up with a vision and S.M.A.R.T. objectives for your relationship is not a simple task. Exploring attitudes about money, branding your relationship, or merging life cultures is not easy either. Neither is writing a relationship job description, giving performance feedback or determining what compensation and benefits you get from the relationship. Finally, meeting to discuss it all every year isn't for the weak-willed or faint of heart.

But I promise you that if you do these things and apply yourself to the best practices in this book, your relationship will flourish in ways that you never imagined. As you have seen, you can create a structure for your relationship in which love, authenticity, and a sense of friendship can thrive unencumbered by problems that typically undermine contemporary relationships founded on failed relationship models of the past.

I believe this is the first book you have read about using the business model as the foundation for marriage. *The*

Business of Love has brought together the two separate worlds of intimate relationships and business. I hope it has made the case for taking a business approach to building your relationship. While these separate worlds are indeed very different, they are comparable in that they require similarly high levels of purposeful effort to make them successful. As history shows, a new model for marriage is sorely needed, and statistics verify that the institution of marriage is in trouble or, as some believe, even broken. *The Business of Love* is my contribution to the transformation of intimate relationships in marriages and families!

Romance vs. intimacy

If you use the nine proven business best practices outlined in this book, you and your partner will have a much more stable, mature relationship than before. You will reach the most satisfying closeness that a couple can achieve: intimacy, and a sense of warmth, closeness, and ease with your life and your partner that allows romance to flourish.

Intimacy is saying, "I know everything about you and I still love and care about you. I am committed to your growth and I support you, as I know you support me. We both make sacrifices for the other so that each of us can have the best relationship possible." When you can honestly say or feel this in your heart, you've reached the highest level of relationship intimacy. Of course, this is not to say that there won't be any challenges in your relationship from here on out, but you now have tools to help negotiate and resolve any issue that might arise!

Revisit the book's main model, using business best practices to improve the bottom line of your relationship. It's a continually renewing model that starts and ends with your vision statement. If you had trouble in the beginning of this book writing and agreeing on a common vision, go back now and make sure you have some sense of what you want your relationship to focus on.

The Business of Love Model

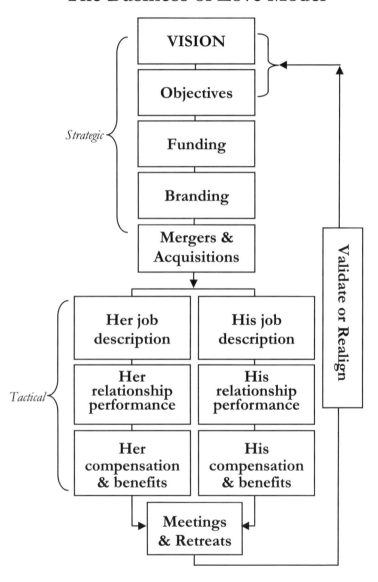

From the vision statement flows a logical set of measurable objectives. Then you are ready to explore attitudes about money, develop and market your marital brand, create detailed job descriptions, provide constructive feedback, determine your emotional paycheck, and hold regular meetings and retreats. Whether you merge or acquire to form your relationship, these best practices from the business world will keep your relationship on the right track!

This is a cause-and-effect world where you get what you give. Think about it: a full-time job means working 2,080 hours a year if you are an hourly worker and, on average, over 2,800 hours if you are salaried. Now, most would agree that your marriage is more important than your job! So, imagine what would happen if you pledged to invest 1/10th of the time you spend on the job working on your relationship. You'll be giving your partner 200 or more hours of relationship time. I don't mean sitting at home watching TV with your partner. Instead, I am asking that you consider how powerful, positive and fulfilling your relationship could be if you both invested this many hours in building and sustaining a world-class marriage.

Free will

You have a choice: You can either accept the poor odds of being in a successful relationship, or you can build an intimate relationship that actually works in today's world. *The Business of Love* means you must be a historian and learn from the past *and* you must be a pioneer and courageously go where no one has gone before, using a radically different approach.

As quoted in a previous chapter, "Love is blind, and marriage is an institution for the blind." Open your eyes, look at yourself in the mirror, and become someone worth spending a lifetime with. A world-class relationship is within your grasp!

Afterword
Dual-Income Couples'
Work/Life Balance
Research

Highlights

As part of my dissertation research, I studied how marital satisfaction of dual-income couples affected their commitment to their employer. A summary of the findings is provided here as further evidence of the need for a new model for relationships (especially dual-income), as described in *The Business of Love*.

169

This was a descriptive research study that involved data collection using a marital satisfaction and an organizational commitment questionnaire. The setting for the study involved 25 organizations that represented the public, private and non-profit sectors. The main question that guided the study was:

What was the relationship between employees' degree of marital satisfaction and their commitment to their current employer?

The relationship between employee and employer is changing at an unprecedented rate and intensity. Concurrently, today's families must cope in a dynamic environment where the definition of what it means to be a family has undergone a permanent transformation. In a single generation, dual-income marriages have gone from being rare to being the norm. These dual-income couples are faced with the typical pressures that can affect any marriage along with a unique set of challenges never faced by any other generation in U.S. history.

Further complicating matters is the fact that there is a growing emphasis on corporate performance often achieved through short-term strategies that include rapid outsourcing of all but "mission critical" jobs, only to have the same employees return as part-time contractors or consultants.

In addition, decades of mergers, acquisitions, layoffs, bankruptcies, off-shoring and outsourcing have shattered employment security and worker commitment. Finally, as social research shows, in post 9/11 America, and in the aftermath of the hurricanes of 2005, the heightened concerns of Baby Boomers, Gen Xers and Gen Ys about divorce, child-rearing and elder care, have developed into a strong sensitivity to quality of work/life issues.

Dual-Income Couples Divorcing Their Employers

This study, along with many others, reveals a very troubling trend among dual-income couples and their level of commitment to their employers. Their response is, in part, to protect their marriages and to spend more time in family activities.

- For these reasons, many of today's best and brightest employees are lowering their career expectations, cutting back on their work hours and actively disengaging from the demands of their jobs despite employers' best efforts to be sensitive, responsive and family-friendly.

- One in three, dual-income employees are placing fixed constraints on the number of hours they will work and 75% of dual-income employees are scaling back career expectations and commitment to work.

- It is no coincidence that this is occurring at a time with the national rate of marriage has dropped 43% in the past 4 decades, and based on some estimates, nearly 1 in 2 marriages fail. In response, many couples are eliminating their previous commitments to their employers in favor of a quality lifestyle featuring less interference from work, placing fixed constraints on the number of hours they work, and reducing disruption in their children's lives by taking a one-career, one-job approach.

Most Employers Are Unaware They Are Losing the Battle

This is happening at a time when Human Resource professionals are struggling with developing appropriate and sustainable strategies to deal with an ever-tightening labor market. Corporate response has been mixed, at best, and despite many high profile attempts to implement an array of family-friendly policies, the actual practice of being family-friendly often fails to achieve meaningful changes in the organization's culture.

Despite claims to the contrary, employees believe that their employer expects them to invest in their jobs first and minimize the intrusion of family obligations. Available research on the negative spillover of work into the home indicates that undesirable effects can be moderated by supportive supervision by employers and by providing employees with greater flexibility and autonomy over their hours of work. Yet, many employers are resistant to accommodating the peculiar nature of the dual-income couples, and many employees believe that allowing children to disrupt work means your career options are diminished.

Fortunately, some companies have established packages

of family-friendly benefits, including flexible scheduling, flextime, and parental leave. These benefits are not so much to accommodate the unique needs of dual-income employees but more as a recruiting tool. There is clear evidence that working parents are attracted to organizations that offer a balance between work and family responsibilities, but once again, there is often a significant gap between policy and practice. While their intentions may be positive, many corporate executives are deceiving themselves if they think that family-friendly programs and polices are improving employee commitment or are worth the investment.

It can become easier to focus on the external family-friendly rankings a company might gain, than it does to make the substantive changes in the organizational culture required to turn policy into practice that employees actually feel and believe. Human Resources executives routinely compete for top rankings in an ever-growing number of corporate contests such as the:

- "100 Best Companies to Work For,"
- "50 Best Small & Medium Companies to Work for in America,"
- "100 Best Companies for Working Mothers,"
- "Top 50 Companies for Diversity,"
- "Best Companies for Women of Color,"
- "50 Best Companies for Latinas,"
- "Best Employers for Workers Over 50,"
- "Best Places to Work in the Federal Government."

While pursuing such recognition is not inherently wrong, it is a flawed strategy. If the practice of being family-friendly is to ever become an engrained part of an organization's culture, the employees are the ones that should be doing the ranking. Top rankings as a family-friendly company may ensure a steady flow of dual-income job seekers, but without establishing a true family-friendly culture, these same individuals, once they become employees, will quickly realize that the policy does not translate to practice… they feel deceived.

Nationwide, over 70% of mothers with children younger than 18 hold down paying jobs and more than one in two mothers with children less than a year old are working. Every one of them had to face that emotionally wrenching return to the workplace after maternity leave, mostly out of economic necessity. Many working mothers employed by Fortune 500 companies frequently avoid requesting flexible scheduling, flextime, or parental leave, because they fear that this will lower their standing for promotions or increase the likelihood of their being laid off.

Perhaps most telling of the gap between family-friendly, human resources policy and practice is that of 384 Fortune 500 companies that extended some type of paternity leave to their male employees, it was found that in total only nine of those companies had received a single request for this benefit. Most male employees are reluctant to take advantage of any family-friendly benefits because they believe it will jeopardize their careers. Even when organizations provide benefits that address work-family conflicts, a significant number of employees fear that they will be seen as less than top performers if they actually use them.

Some Employers Are Becoming Enlightened

This and other studies are creating a better understanding of how family-friendly, human resource policies and practices can affect marital satisfaction of dual-income workers. In turn, this can increase the commitment of these employees as measured by their motivation, contribution, energy, time and productivity. The results provide insight for employers dealing with the affect of key workplace trends that are creating unprecedented challenges for corporate executives, in terms of finding and keeping talented employees in a dynamic business environment.

Enlightened executives, who focus on the organization's culture, are in a unique position to examine the real value of their existing family-friendly policies and develop innovative Human Resource strategies to positively affect the lives of their employees and not simply compete for rankings in a popularity contest. Family-friendly benefits could be identified that are meaningful, worth the investment, and are actually used by employees. Human Resource executives will have a competitive advantage in attracting the growing scarcity of the best and brightest workers who can be equally committed to family and career, if they have an employer who supports both.

Additional research is needed to fully explore the relatively unstudied relationship between employee commitment and marital satisfaction. The currently available data about the relationship between organizational commitment and marital satisfaction of dual-income couples has not produced clear findings about the strength of that relationship, whether it is positive or negative, or the influence of demographic and job-related variables upon the relationship.

It is anticipated that additional research will have theoretical and practical significance that would represent a meaningful addition to the existing data about dual-income families in general, and about the relationship between marital satisfaction and organizational commitment, in particular. Also, there appears to be few studies that assess the influence of demographic variables such as gender and age upon the strength of the relationship between marital satisfaction and organizational commitment.

This type of research may also be useful in determining the value of current family-friendly work policies, in modifying those policies to reduce work/family conflict, and in identifying those workers who are most likely to benefit from family-friendly policies or those who might suffer most from the absence of family-friendly policies.

Finally, additional research into the various theories about the implications of work/life balance might lead to the development of a new understanding about the evolving work-family facilitation model. Unlike most previous research that assumes work and family are in conflict, the facilitation model views work and family as complimentary. Previous models were pre-disposed to view the new phenomena of dual-income couples as negative. The explosion of dual-income couples in the past few decades was seen as disruptive and in contrast to the traditional family with one parent, usually the mother, not working outside of the home. Now, however, more study is needed to gauge the long-term influence on work and family since dual-income couples have become the norm in our society and in the workforce.

APPENDIX

THE BUSINESS OF LOVE - QUESTIONS

1. I am reading *The Business of Love* but can't get my wife to read it or do any of the exercises in the workbook. Do you have any suggestions?

   One core belief of the book is that to have a successful relationship, you must first BE the right person, not try to FIND the right person. While it is certainly helpful to have both you and your wife reading the book at the same time, all too often the focus of relationship development is to get your partner to change. This book is about you, first work on yourself to be a good relationship role model, and worry about your wife later.

2. I have always been a stay-at-home mom and wondered if a non-business person like me can understand *The Business of Love*?

   The concepts in the book are universal and do not require any type of business or work background. The book explains each "Best Practice" in a way that anyone can understand and apply. I think, for example, that the need for clear job descriptions to help you and your husband avoid conflicts about household chores is intuitive and universally understood.

3. Will *The Business of Love* help me if I have been married for over 25 years?

   I do not believe that the length of the relationship matters. In a long-term relationship, the "Best Practices" in the book may provide a concrete way to explain what is working well in your marriage after all those years. In addition, it could provide clear directions on how to focus on new areas that you may want to address to deepen your relationship.

4. I have dragged my husband to marriage counseling but I wonder if he can be helped by reading *The Business of Love* instead?

This is not a therapy book to fix his or your dysfunctional past or a deeply troubled relationship. Instead, it's written for normal men and women who are smart enough to know that love alone will not make a relationship last. I think the book has very broad application and can be used as a simple way to figure out why you are in counseling. It can also be helpful in rebuilding a rocky relationship by using the "Best Practices" to address those things that you may have overlooked in the beginning of the marriage.

5. I am working full time and have two pre-school age children, so how do you think I can find time to read the book or complete *The Business of Love* exercises?

You should find that the book is quick and easy reading. The 9 "Best Practices" chapters in the book are designed to be completed in the order in which they are presented but can also work quite well as stand-alone chapters. So, if you're limited on time, consider scanning the Table of Contents to find the "Best Practice" that seems most relevant. In addition, you can find a quick overview of the "Best Practices" at www.thebusinessoflove.org or simply try an exercise or two from *The Business of Love* Workbook. One big advantage is that if you have a job, then you likely already know most of the "Best Practices" in the book. The only thing new is to consider using them in your intimate relationship.

6. I am 26 and single and wondered if you think I can get anything out of reading *The Business of Love*?

APPENDIX

Most everyone is either in a relationship, or is trying to get into one or out of one. If you're single, *The Business of Love* can be quite useful in figuring out what may have gone wrong with previous relationships, and what to look for and guard against in order to and to prepare for successful relationships in the future.

7. I just reluctantly ended my third marriage but read everything I could find to try to avoid another failed marriage. So why is *The Business of Love* any better than other self-help relationship books?

I don't know if it is better, but I assure you it is different. As the book points out, marriage is not working, in part, because many relationships are based on failed models of the past. Most existing self-help books try to address how to fix relationships built on models that no longer work. In light of all your other reading, perhaps it's time for a radically different approach, and that is what *The Business of Love* is all about.

8. I may be a hopeless romantic and want an impossible fantasy relationship, but I can't understand how you can mix business with an intimate relationship in *The Business of Love?*

I don't necessarily see it as mixing as much as providing a brand new basis for relationships. The key in teaching something new is to be able to link it to something you already know. The business concepts that comprise the "Best Practices" in the book are common concepts that most anyone would already know from working in any type of job setting. Most importantly, this book is all about romance, intimacy and how to ensure that a loving relationship continues to grow.

9. While reading *The Business of Love,* I realized that I should have never married my spouse in the first place… now what?

As I caution from the beginning, the book may be very unsettling as you explore new information about yourself and your partner. Without knowing more details, it is hard for me to say that the relationship is over. If you do not see eye-to-eye regarding job descriptions, for example, that might be relatively easy to overcome. If, on the other hand, you do not share the same long-term vision for the future, then you may have made a mistake. If this is the case, at least now you know it and have a more constructive means to describe why you fear it is over without blaming and attacking your spouse.

10. I think that I am a very controlling person and as I read *The Business of Love,* my biggest fear is that I will lose control of my marriage. Help?

I think that trying to control a partner in a relationship is the opposite of intimacy. But it is also important to remember that control in a marriage is not necessarily a bad thing, if you and your partner first agree to who has control over what. For example, in *The Business of Love* I describe the role of clear job descriptions to spell out, up-front, who has control over what. In this context, it simply means that control of a particular task or duty around the house is given to the person who is most motivated and competent at performing it. In this context, control is shared and not fought over.

THE BUSINESS OF LOVE
Best Practices & Stages of Relationship Checklist

The following provides an overview of the stages that all intimate relationships will experience. Many relationships do not make it past the Conflict Stage, but for those who do, it may be possible to build the foundation during the Resolution Stage to achieve a truly Intimate Relationship. Use this checklist as a quick reference to identify which stage you think your relationship is in and what are the most appropriate Best Practices to successful navigate through that stage.

Five Stages of Relationships

STAGE	1) ROMANCE
Description	This is the 1st stage of a new relationship. Each person is often on their best behavior & wanting the approval of their new partner. It is a time of dating, perhaps physical intimacy & an opportunity to get better acquainted.
Key Emotions	excitement enthusiasm "turned on" caring
Characteristics	fantasies dreams anticipation illusions
Behavior	approving, cooperative, supportive, accepting sensitivity, warmth, closeness, understanding
Challenges	getting started with careers entertaining others determining competencies, expenses of dating, leisure time values
Best Practice(s) Needed	Creating the Vision

Five Stages of Relationships	
STAGE	**2) COMMITMENT**
Description	This is the 2nd stage of an evolving relationship. Each person often decides on his or her own, or jointly to become exclusive & monogamous. Each partner has what they feel & sense is a good grasp of the other person's habits, values & behavior.
Key Emotions	hopeful focused anticipation loving
Characteristics	practical exclusive publicly an "item" attached predictable accessibility
Behavior	open displays of affection, terms of endearment family activities, relatives involved intimacy, sensitivity, partnership in planning
Challenges	blending families career decisions, power issues a "sense of us" new traditions, not losing self
Best Practice(s) Needed	Creating the Vision Developing Objectives Funding Branding Mergers & Acquisitions

Five Stages of Relationships	
STAGE	**3) CONFLICT**
Description	This 3rd stage of the evolving relationship is when the fantasy & illusions disappear. Each person may feel they "have" the other. They are no longer on their best behavior. Other priorities & issues such as values, sex, money, power, children, work, leisure & communication become the new challenges.
Key Emotions	frustration disappointment fear anxiety pressure doubt
Characteristics	distance protective defensive avoidance
Behavior	blaming, less closeness, fewer shared activities accepting, consoling, understanding, tolerance
Challenges	money, career choices dominance & control child rearing intimacy
Best Practice(s) Needed	Funding Branding Mergers & Acquisitions Job Descriptions Relationship Feedback Compensation & Benefits

Five Stages of Relationships	
STAGE	**4) RESOLUTION**
Description	This 4th stage of a relationship is marked with a wide variety of attempts to stabilize the rocky relationship. Couples may try outlets such as work, kids & other outside activities. Some couples may start to talk & find that improved communication re-stores the stability they desire.
Key Emotions	anger sadness depression panic hope resignation anticipation
Characteristics	analytical roles & duties distance pre-occupied
Behavior	lack of concern, insensitivity, distance, self-oriented, unavailable acceptance, understanding resolution
Challenges	value conflicts, control, power, money intimacy, communication leisure, children work
Best Practice(s) Needed	Mergers & Acquisitions Job Descriptions Relationship Feedback Compensation & Benefits Meetings & Retreats

Five Stages of Relationships	
STAGE	**5) INTIMACY**
Description	This 5th stage of a relationship is the start of a period of stability. The couple has learned to communicate & resolve conflicts in a win-win manner. Romance will often re-surface. Each sees the other with all their faults & shortcomings & they still like each other. They both feel they made a good choice.
Key Emotions	love warmth empathy understanding accepting
Characteristics	fun light-hearted mutual respect shared & parallel activities
Behavior	touching, other focused, interested sensitive, accepting, tolerant loving, interested, supportive
Challenges	children work, money leisure
Best Practice(s) Needed	Job Descriptions Relationship Feedback Compensation & Benefits Meetings & Retreats

VERBAL INTIMACY CHECKLIST:
How we avoid intimacy by the way we talk!

In order to learn about connecting with one another in healthy ways, we must first examine the rules we have learned to avoid closeness in our personal relationships. The following is a checklist for assessing habits you might want to break. Check all that apply to your typical communication patterns.

❑ Always say "you" or "it" instead of "I."

❑ If someone says something personal to you, joke about it or laugh.

❑ Try to maintain topical discussions. Talk about "safe" subjects like weather, sports, or current events, where little personal disclosure is made. The language is usually in the form of "it" or "they."

❑ If someone takes an emotional risk with you, ignore it or change the subject. If someone states they like something you did or they want to get to know you better, do not acknowledge their reaching out to you.

❑ If you like someone, tell another person instead of the one you like. Be indirect.

❑ Never talk openly with a family member or close friend about your relationship with him or her, especially if you are alone together.

❑ Avoid being alone with the person who you are supposed to be intimate with. Escape any opportunities for closeness. If you are alone, bring up another person - or cause - to talk about.

❑ Don't disclose any strong feelings of loving, caring, loneliness, sadness, or fear.

❑ Never acknowledge any pain from your past; keep it secret.

❑ Protect yourself from who you really are; turn to others to define you. Fulfill *others'* expectations of you, not your own.

❑ Don't risk being vulnerable or unprotected. If you hear about someone's vulnerability, be sure to gossip to others about it or store it to use against the person later for revenge.

❑ Stay busy; fill up with chatter, alcohol, food, work, and things. You won't have to feel lonely.

RELATIONSHIP EFFECTIVENESS SURVEY

On a scale of 1-4, please circle the number that indicates your level of disagreement or agreement with each of the statements below.

Statements	*Disagree---Agree*
1. Roles & responsibilities in our relationship are clear.	1-----2-----3-----4
2. Our relationship has an effective problem-solving process.	1-----2-----3-----4
3. Both partners actively participate in decisions affecting us.	1-----2-----3-----4
4. Our relationship responds well to change.	1-----2-----3-----4
5. We can discuss our ideas & concerns openly with each other.	1-----2-----3-----4
6. Each partner is sensitive to the feelings & needs of the other.	1-----2-----3-----4
7. Each partner sets a good example to inspire cooperation of the other.	1-----2-----3-----4
8. Our relationship has a clear vision & objectives.	1-----2-----3-----4
9. We each look beyond our own needs to focus on the relationship.	1-----2-----3-----4
10. As partners, we work well together.	1-----2-----3-----4
11. There is a high level of trust between us.	1-----2-----3-----4
12. Our relationship recognizes & utilizes the strengths of each partner.	1-----2-----3-----4
13. Responsibilities within the relationship are distributed appropriately.	1-----2-----3-----4
14. I am proud to be a partner in this relationship.	1-----2-----3-----4
15. Overall, I rate the effectiveness of our relationship as excellent.	1-----2-----3-----4
16. What is the one thing that most needs to change for the relationship to be even better?	

RELATIONSHIP COMMUNICATION
SKILLS INVENTORY

Attending Behavior - *physically and non-verbally giving total psychological attention to your partner*

A. Strong points as viewed by you and by your partner...

　　1.

　　2.

B. Weak points as viewed by you and by your partner...

　　1.

　　2.

Listening Skills – *making it safe for your partner to talk*

A. Strong points as viewed by you and by your partner...

　　1.

　　2.

B. Weak points as viewed by you and by your partner...

　　1.

　　2.

Confrontation – addresses difficult issues constructively

A. Place a check on the following continuum describing your typical confrontation style with the following:

Stranger:
Passive ------- Assertive/Expressive --------- Aggressive/Explosive

Family:
Passive ------- Assertive/Expressive --------- Aggressive/Explosive

Partner:
Passive ------- Assertive/Expressive ---------- Aggressive/Explosive

190

APPENDIX

Overall discomfort with confronting others - circle number:

	No Discomfort	-	Moderate	-	High Discomfort
Stranger:	1	2	3	4	5
Family:	1	2	3	4	5
Partner:	1	2	3	4	5

A. Strong points in confrontation as viewed by you and by your partner...

    1.

    2.

B. Weak points in confrontation as viewed by you and by your partner...

    1.

    2.

Problem Solving Style

A. Place a check on continuum describing your typical problem solving style:

Stranger:
Permissive --------------- *Democratic* --------------- *Authoritarian*

Family:
Permissive --------------- *Democratic* --------------- *Authoritarian*

Partner:
Permissive --------------- *Democratic* --------------- *Authoritarian*

B. Strong points in problem solving as viewed by you and by your partner...

    1.

    2.

C. Weak points in problem solving as viewed by you and by your partner...

    1.

    2.

LISTENING SKILLS:
How to listen so others will talk!

1. Silence

The listener's willingness to keep quiet and let the person tell his or her story.

Examples: Eye contact or nodding your head

2. Acknowledgement Responses

Sends a message that the listener is following the sender's story.

Examples: "I see." "Mm-hmmm"

3. Door Openers

The listener sends an invitation of willingness to listen.

Examples: "Tell me more."
"What can I do to help?"
"Could you provide some more details?"

4. Active Listening

This assures the sender that the listener understands the message; a check on the listener's impression of the sender's expression.

Example: Any restatement in the listener's own words of the sender's message; feedback.

APPENDIX

RESPONDING SKILLS:
Talking so others <u>don't</u> listen!

1. Conventional - small talk, chit-chat

Necessary and appropriate conversation that is the majority of all talking, i.e. "Hi, how are you?"; "Isn't this weather great?"; "What'd you think about the game?"; "Did you get the car fixed?"

2. Defensive - protect, conceal, avoid

- ❑ *Blamer:* attacks, blames not responsible for their own actions.
- ❑ *Placator:* apologizes, tries to evoke guilt, hard to confront.
- ❑ *Reasoner:* logical, rational, analytical and awkward with feelings.
- ❑ *Irrelevant*: dodges issues, changes subject, impossible to pin down.

COMMUNICATION SKILLS:
Talking so others <u>will</u> listen!

3. Door Openers - an invitation to have a more honest conversation and resolve conflict

Explorative attempts to talk about a subject that may be awkward or difficult to discuss.

4. Leveling - open, honest and non-judgmental conversation

Open, honest and objective disclosure of thoughts, feelings, and opinions. Acting in a self-responsible manner in an attempt to discuss someone's behavior and to resolve conflict. Can be summarized as: "I feel... about... because..."

ELEMENTS OF RELATIONSHIP TEAMWORK

Rate your relationship on the elements by circling the appropriate number on each line.

How clear are the objectives of the relationship?
(Objectives are the degree by which it is clear how actions & activities are directed towards an individual or series of specific targets to improve or sustain the relationship.)

1	2	3	4	5
No apparent objectives	Objectives are unclear in conflict	Average clarity of objectives	Objectives mostly clear	Objectives very clear

How much trust & openness is in the relationship?
(Talking honestly without fear of consequences leads to trust & trust is the faith in self & your partner to do the right thing for the relationship.)

1	2	3	4	5
Distrust & no openness	Little trust but some openness	Average trust & openness	Significant trust & openness	Remarkable trust & openness

How empathetic are partners to each other?
(How well do both partners in the relationship understand & identify with the concerns, problems & accomplishments of the other?)

1	2	3	4	5
No empathy	Little empathy	Average empathy	Considerable empathy	Remarkable empathy

APPENDIX

How much attention is paid to process & content?

(The way a relationship is working. How the relationship works is as important as what is achieved. The end does not justify the means if it damages the relationship.)

1	2	3	4	5
No attention to process or content	Little attention to process & content	Some concern with process & content	A fair balance between process & content	Very concerned with process & content

How are relationship leadership needs met?

(Leadership in a relationship means the ability of one partner to rally behind the other based on their skills or abilities.)

1	2	3	4	5
Not met, drifting	Leadership driven by one partner	Some leadership sharing	Leadership functions distributed	Leadership needs met creatively

How are relationship decisions made?

(Do the partners make choices based on what is best for the relationship, thereby building consensus, or do power struggles occur & win-lose decisions happen?)

1	2	3	4	5
Unable to reach decisions	Decisions made by one person	Decisions made by random means	Attempts at integrating both partner's wishes	Full partner consensus

STRESS PREVENTION CHECKLIST

There can be a fine line between stress that powers performance and keeps us focused and distress that can damage or even destroy the healthiest relationship. Review the following list of ways to prevent normal stress from becoming overwhelming and disabling. Please check any prevention techniques that you are using on a regular basis, or are thinking about implementing in your daily life and in your relationship.

❑ **Get Strokes.** Ask for recognition & appreciation from your partner.

❑ **Enhance Your Environment.** Make changes in your physical environment to make it more pleasing and comfortable for you.

❑ **Manage Your Physical Health.** Take responsibility for your physical well-being through exercise, proper diet, and adequate rest.

❑ **Establish Support Systems.** Develop a support system of people beyond your partner who really care about you as a person.

❑ **Manage Your Time.** The only time we ever really have is NOW. Release the past, don't dwell on the future, do what is at hand.

❑ **Stack the Deck in Your Favor.** When possible, take on those tasks and chores in the relationship that you enjoy and with which you will likely be successful.

❑ **Take Time Out for Leisure.** Engage in a truly mindless activity in which you can be completely removed from your usual roles as partner, parent or employee.

❑ **Set Limits and Learn to Say "No."** Accept only those problems and responsibilities that are truly yours.

❑ **Use Humor to Lighten the Load.** Learn to laugh at yourself. "Angels can fly because they take themselves lightly."

❑ **Be Willing to Take Risks.** Don't be afraid to stick your neck out a little; be open to new ideas or a different approach that your partner might suggest.

❑ **Don't Expect Perfection.** Know and respect your own and your partner's limits in terms of skills, energy, dedication and commitment.

❑ **Nurture Your Relationships.** Maintain a profound connection to your partner. Be tethered to something and someone of great significance in your life.

STRESS "RED FLAG" SYMPTOM CHECKLIST

The following is a checklist of 12 "Red Flag" symptoms for assessing your stress level. Circle the number that indicates your current level of intensity with each Red Flag. Use this checklist whenever you feel your stress level rising to help you recognize when you are becoming overloaded.

Level of Intensity	Low--------High
1. **Personal Habits -** *Changes in regular sleeping, eating, or exercise routines*	1 - 2 - 3 - 4
2. **Clutter -** *Undone things are screaming at you; everything is priority #1*	1 - 2 - 3 - 4
3. **Feeling Pushed -** *Owned by the clock; having physical symptoms, i.e., headaches, etc.*	1 - 2 - 3 - 4
4. **Feeling Indispensable -** *Can't say "no;" caught in the need-to-be-needed cycle*	1 - 2 - 3 - 4
5. **No Joy in Life -** *Everything about life, work or the relationship is a problem*	1 - 2 - 3 - 4
6. **Professional Martyr -** *Working harder, but accomplishing less; life-style choices suffer*	1 - 2 - 3 - 4
7. **Substance Abuse -** *Using food, alcohol, nicotine, etc. to cope*	1 - 2 - 3 - 4
8. **Preoccupation or Absentmindedness -** *Lost in thought, daydreaming*	1 - 2 - 3 - 4
9. **Chronic Trouble in Relationships -** *unresolved problems in personal relations*	1 - 2 - 3 - 4
10. **Boredom -** *Loss of interest in job, friends, family & outside activities*	1 - 2 - 3 - 4
11. **Emotional Roller Coaster -** *Caught in a cycle of anxiety, frustration, anger and depression*	1 - 2 - 3 - 4
12. **Wanting to Run Away -** *Fantasies about escaping or dropping out*	1 - 2 - 3 - 4

Total your scores from all 12 Red Flags. If your score is more than 24, it may be time to back off and re-emphasize prevention strategies or look at ways to recover.

STRESS RECOVERY CHECKLIST

The following is a checklist of a step-by-step process of recovery, if or when you discover that you are living in a state of chronic distress and have burned out!

1. **Stop Fighting.** Admit that you're "burned out." Tell your partner and your support system. No problem can be solved until it is acknowledged.

2. **Simplify.** Find a place where you can be quiet and still, and stay there until the confusion in your mind begins to settle down.

3. **Re-evaluate Choices.** Once you begin to calm down, evaluate your lifestyle and see what is contributing to your happiness, and what is detracting from it.

4. **Adjust Your Expectations.** Take an inventory of the expectations you have regarding yourself, your relationship and your career.

5. **Get More Training.** Upgrade your life coping skills, whether related to the job or to your role as a spouse or parent.

6. **Shift Responsibilities.** Look into the lateral moves that may be available to you within your current organization or with your partner in the home.

7. **Take Some Time Off.** Engage in a truly mindless activity in which you can be completely out of your role.

8. **Seek Professional Help.** Personal or career counseling may be in order.

9. **Quit.** Consider that it may be time to take the big risk and move on to something (or someone) else.

APPENDIX

CREATIVE RELATIONSHIP PROBLEM SOLVING

1. Recognize and agree that a problem exists.

Do not assume that your partner is affected by the same problem. To solve a problem in the relationship, you must both recognize and agree that a problem exists.

2. Define the problem.

In many instances what appears to be the problem is, in fact, a symptom. Be sure to clearly define the problem in concise and specific terms or it will probably recur in a different form.

3. Generate possible solutions.

It is important at this step to remember that the creativity necessary to generate possible solutions is very different than evaluating those solutions. DO NOT develop one solution and then analyze it; instead, simply write it down and move on to the next possible solution.

4. Evaluate solutions and select the best one.

This step involves the evaluation process and should be viewed as a discussion and not simply a quick process of elimination. Each possible solution should now be thoroughly examined in light of what is best for the relationship. Consider these specific criteria: What will it cost? How much time will it take? How obvious are the benefits? How relevant is it to the problem? How visible is the solution? What impact might it have on others? Are there any pitfalls?

5. Create a plan to implement the solution.

This step involves the creation of a specific plan to ensure that the solution chosen is fully implemented. Remember to communicate the implementation plan to all who will be affected. Be sure to follow-up and evaluate the solution to ensure that the problem is being reduced or eliminated.

CREATIVE PROBLEM-SOLVING ACTION PLAN

Partners & others present:			
Problem addressed:			
Decisions made / actions to be taken	Who	Due	Result
1)			
2)			
3)			
4)			
5)			

APPENDIX

BEHAVIORAL CONTRACT

Select one behavior change that you identified while reading **The Business of Love** *that you could make to improve your relationship. Next, write a detailed and specific plan as to how you will make this change in your daily behavior with your partner.*

1. Behavior change that you want to implement:

2. What are some specific examples of this behavior change – what will it "look like?"

   •

   •

3. When will you implement this behavior change?

   • Date you will start:
   • Well underway by....
   • Date you would like to accomplish these actions:

4. How will you get feedback from your partner to ensure that you are implementing the behavior change that you have committed to in this contract?

5. Please sign and date this contract, then ask your partner to support you in the successful completion of this contract. Ask him or her to witness this contract and agree to a time that the two of you will check with each other to see how well you are doing in fulfilling this contract.

Sign _____ Date_____

Witness _____ Checkup Date_____